FAIR ISLE
Knitting Tradition

FAIR ISLE KNITTING TRADITION

Landauer Publishing, www.landauerpub.com, is an imprint of Fox Chapel Publishing Company, Inc.

Project Team
Acquisitions Editor: Amelia Johanson
Technical Editor: Heather Storta
Editor: Christa Oestreich
Designer: Leslie Hall
Photographer: Kevin Theakston
Proofreader: Jeremy Hauck
Indexer: Jay Kreider

Shutterstock used: ViSnezh (geometric design, used throughout); RedKoala (line design, 7, 9, 17, 22, 26, 29, 51, 70, 152); wirakorn deelert (old paper, back cover); danler (Fair Isle graphic, back cover).

ISBN 978-1-63981-106-9

Library of Congress Control Number: 2025936691

To learn more about the other great books from Fox Chapel Publishing, or to find a retailer near you, call toll-free at 800-457-9112 or visit us at www.FoxChapelPublishing.com.
You can also send mail to:
Fox Chapel Publishing
903 Square Street
Mount Joy, PA 17552

We are always looking for talented authors.
To submit an idea, please send a brief inquiry to acquisitions@foxchapelpublishing.com.

Printed in China
First printing

FAIR ISLE
Knitting Tradition

›»○«‹

SHETLAND HERITAGE PATTERNS FOR STUNNING SWEATERS, HATS, SOCKS, AND GLOVES

ALISON RENDALL

TABLE OF CONTENTS

PART 1:
ORIGINS

INTRODUCTION

My great-great-grandmother is pictured here in a traditional Shetland "butt and ben" croft house of the late 19th century.

This photo shows the "ganseys" (sweaters) my mother knitted for my sister and me in the 1970s.

My name is Alison Rendall. I am a Shetlander born and bred. Likewise, both sides of my family are rooted in the Shetland Islands— an archipelago belonging to Scotland, located between Scotland and Norway—for many generations. As a child in the early 1970s, I watched my mother, grandmother, and others around me knitting constantly. Therefore, knitting was an intrinsic part of the fabric of everyday Shetland life to the point that learning to knit was classed as an essential skill and formed part of the school curriculum. Although I was taught to knit Fair Isle by my grandmother, I was lucky enough to also receive knitting lessons at school. I looked forward to these weekly lessons—a welcome break from math and spelling. My mother knitted new *ganseys* for me and my sister each year as we grew. "Gansey" is the Shetland word for a woolen sweater. (For authenticity, I will continue to refer to Shetland words throughout the text. A glossary is provided on page 11.)

Shetland has a long, rich history of textiles, and knitting has played an important part in the livelihood of Shetland families like my own. At the very least, it enabled folk to make warm clothes for their families, but for many, it offered a trade for the rest of their lives. Additionally, knitting provided essential supplementary income in a pre–oil industry era when there was much less affluence.

After the oil boom of the 1970s, folk were drawn into the far more lucrative salaries of the oil industry. Traditional croft houses gave way to larger houses and increasing lack of interest in Shetland knitwear meant that cottage industry knitters reduced significantly.

Despite these changes, the traditional craft of knitting in Shetland persisted and has since revived itself. The Shetland schools continued to teach Fair Isle knitting until very recently, and even now there are volunteers ensuring that youngsters still have the chance to learn the craft. Slowly but surely, interest in Shetland history and culture and its associated knitting began to gain interest. The Shetland Textile Museum was established in 1996 by the Shetland Guild of Spinners, Knitters, Weavers, and Dyers. The museum is active in conserving examples of Shetland textiles from 19th century to present day and displaying various tools and equipment used in knitting. People from all over the world visit both the Shetland Museum & Archives and the Textile Museum to witness the impressive knitwear collections they house.

In 2010, Shetland Wool Week was established to help with the revival of the Shetland textile industry, which produced some of the finest lace and Fair Isle knitwear in the world. In promoting and celebrating Shetland wool from the United Kingdom's most northerly native sheep, the festival attracted folk who were interested in learning from generations of skilled, hardworking knitters and crofters (farmers) in Shetland. Shetland Wool Week has flourished into an internationally renowned event and continues to grow each year. Today, thousands of knitting fans from all over the world participate in classes and workshops, visit exhibitions, and generally immerse themselves in the Shetland way of life.

It is wonderful to see Shetland knitting, once borne of necessity, get the respect it deserves. Shetland *makkers* (knitters) now have the chance to share their skills and knowledge on a global scale.

This book features a how-to-knit Fair Isle section (page 29), followed by a collection of 14 Fair Isle designs based on some of the traditional and heritage patterns of Shetland. I'd like to mention that the techniques used in this book are my own, many of them passed down to me through my family. Other makkers in Shetland will have variations on how it is done. This is my first collection of patterns to be made available. The range starts with a simple purse in three colors and progresses up in technical difficulty, ending in a traditional Shetland gansey.

I was proud to be Patron of Shetland Wool Week in 2023 and had the opportunity to share my island's heritage, culture, and artistry with the rest of the world.

LANGUAGE

Shetland was colonized by Viking settlers in the nineth century, establishing Norn as the predominant language within the isles. (This language was exclusively spoken by people in northern Scotland and the islands off the northern coast. It is now extinct.) In 1469, Shetland was pledged to Scotland by Christian I of Denmark as part of a dowry when his daughter, Margaret, became engaged to James III of Scotland. Over time, Shetlanders switched to speaking Scots, although many remained bilingual and continued to speak Norn among themselves. Today, Shetland's language is a melting pot of Norn, Scots, and English words. However, much of its grammar is entirely unrelated to Scots or English. Shetlanders are immensely proud of their Norse roots; therefore, Norn still survives in many of the words we use. This can be seen particularly in place, animal, and bird names as well as crofting and fishing words.

Signs displaying place names in Shetland include each name's origins.

Additionally, many of our makkin words stem from old Norn. As Shetland native industry skills and knitting techniques are passed down from generation to generation, the words themselves are simultaneously, incidentally preserved.

Use of the Shetland language has become diluted over time, with many of our words becoming less used to the point of extinction. To help reverse this trend, I like to use Shetland words in my designs to support Shetland's language and culture. I believe that the practice of integrating these words helps keep them alive both in usage and understanding, bringing them back into the forefront of people's minds.

GLOSSARY OF SHETLAND TERMS

Brak an eke—Knit to the end of the row. At the end of each row, the yarns are broken and rejoined at the start to work another right-side row (see page 45).

Butt and Ben—A traditional croft house, consisting of two rooms.

Cloo—A ball of wool.

Dressing—The finishing process of washing and stretching (blocking) a garment (see page 48).

Kishie—A traditional, handmade straw basket that is worn on the back. It is used for carrying goods, especially peats from the peat hill to the home.

Gansey—A sweater.

Graft—Using Kitchener stitch to join two pieces of knitting together (see page 42).

Hentilaget—A small bit of wool left by a sheep on a fence or on the ground.

Laying on—Casting on (see page 34).

Lightsome—Light-hearted or cheery. Can refer to a person or a good time.

Loop—Stitch.

Makkin—Knitting.

Makkers—Knitters.

Makkin belt—Knitting belt (see page 31).

Oo—Wool.

Peerie—Small.

Roo—To pluck the wool off a sheep.

Spret—To pull back knitting by several rows or more.

Sweerie geng—The first row knitted.

Wastside—West side.

Wires—Double-pointed knitting needles.

Wirset—Yarn that has been spun and is ready to use.

ORIGINS OF FAIR ISLE KNITTING

Fair Isle is a small island with a large history.

Due to the geographical location of Shetland, the islands have always been busy with visitors. Their location places them on a historic Viking sea route stretching from Scandinavia to Greenland. The isles remained active as harbors during the days when ships were the dominant form of transport.

Fair Isle is one of Shetland's islands and lies 24 miles (39km) to the southwest of the Shetland mainland. Fair Isle knitting started on this small island around the 1850s. It is unclear where the influence for patterned knitting came from, but local knowledge suggests that textiles brought back from foreign places inspired women to create and develop their own designs, perhaps because of the established trade routes. Among the original Fair Isle patterns were 17 row motifs with six-sided, lozenge-shaped designs linked together with crosses, called the OXO patterns. Shetland mainland knitters were already experts in fine lace shawls and veils. Around 1910, stranded colorwork (also called Fair Isle knitting) became popular all over Shetland mainland, not solely Fair Isle itself. It is said that the original patterns were copied on scraps of paper and passed from croft to croft and family to family. This led to experimentation with pattern and color. New motifs were added in great number, with different communities in Shetland developing their own unique style. Influence on Shetland knitting has come from far and wide. For example, World War II

Maritime trade was important for bringing new skills and techniques to Shetland.

saw large influxes of Norwegian refugees to Shetland that resulted in the incorporation of large Norwegian star motifs into Shetland knitwear. This influence also saw the start of designs with vertical panels instead of horizontal bands.

Although Fair Isle knitting started in Fair Isle, these days there is little or no distinction between the knitting of Fair Isle and the rest of the Shetland Islands. After 1910, Shetlanders developed our own current range of classic heritage motifs, some based on the old Fair Isle designs, but with the addition of many more. The term "Fair Isle" should be reserved for all the traditional and characteristic patterns of Shetland.

Here is an example of an OXO pattern, used in Hentilagets Hat (page 88).

Sheep are an important part of Fair Isle, providing the wool that locals use for makkin.

Knitting in Shetland was traditionally done by hand and considered very labor intensive. In the past, in rural communities, most people had their own sheep and would therefore produce their own wool. However, it had to be cleaned, teased, hand carded, spun, and plied before they could start knitting with it, not to mention dyeing as part of the process as well. This job was often done by groups of women in the evening after the day's work was done. The gatherings of several generations of women along with friends from neighboring crofts were often sociable and lightsome times.

In the 19th century, the barter system (known as the truck system) meant that Shetland knitters could only trade their knitting in a local shop for goods, not receiving payment. However, this system was unfair and always weighted in favor of the merchant, with the knitter often receiving very little for their hard work. The goods given by the merchant were not necessarily the ones needed, so folk then would have to trade those goods with others to get the items they did need. Cash was usually not an option, but if the knitter was given money, they would be given considerably less in value than if paid in goods.

Investigations into the truck system by a Royal Commission started in 1871, but unbelievably, it took another 70 years before it was finally eradicated. After World War II, Shetlanders were finally freed from the truck system thanks to organizations like the Shetland Hand Knitting Organization. This scheme was set up to protect the interests of Shetland hand knitters and included setting standards and correct marketing for Shetland wool products. This meant that knitters were finally able to obtain more realistic payments for their hand knitting.

Wool continued to be spun by hand at home, but it was recognized that the amounts of wool produced did not match the demand. After World War II, Shetlanders had the option to send their fleeces directly to mainland Scotland for spinning and dyeing, having limited choice in the colors that were sent back to them. Machine processing of the wool increased production of the finished knitted goods by cutting out the need for hand carding and spinning, allowing much more time to be spent on knitting.

It is ironic that, after years of knitting poverty, the period where hand knitting became more valued and better priced was short. By the 1950s and 1960s, hand knitting gave way to machine knitting, which was clearly faster and cheaper to produce. Many women were employed in this knitwear industry, either in a factory making garments or at home finishing them. There were several knitting factories in Shetland where women worked on machines to export plain sweaters in a single color of Shetland wool. Sometimes the factories made sweater bodies on the machines and women at home added in bands of Fair Isle at the cuffs or in the yoke.

A local woman who worked in a knitwear factory in Lerwick in the 1960s described to me how hard she worked. The factory operated in piecework, meaning that she was paid according to the amount she produced rather than by the hour. Being a motivated and capable machinist, she sometimes produced four times the number of items than others. After she left work to get married and have children, her employer felt the loss of his top employee so much that they sent one of the knitting machines to her rural home many miles away to keep up production. Others were able to buy machines and worked from home.

It was also common for fishermen to contribute in the winter months when the weather was poor and there was less time at sea. For example, to make a Fair Isle yoke, it was sometimes the men who would work the main body by machine and then the women would add in the Fair Isle yoke by hand to complete the garment. I think many Shetland children of this era will remember their parents being engrossed in the strenuous effort of pushing the knitting machine carriage endlessly back and forth, along with the unmistakable sound and the wool fluff that goes with it!

My grandmother received a bag of plain sweater sections each week. Her job was to finish the garments by grafting on the neckband and cuffs. It had to be done precisely and carefully so that the seams were invisible. She complained greatly every time the manufacturer sent her a bag of dark colors, as it was much more tiring on the eyes!

After the oil boom, knitting was no longer a necessity, and some were glad to be free of it. However, Shetland women carried on knitting through choice rather than necessity, most often knitting for family members. Some continued in the knitwear industry, setting up small businesses at home and opting to knit Fair Isle with the newly introduced two-color knitting machines. Machine-knitted Fair Isle is made in flat pieces then sewn together, so it is usually straightforward to tell the difference between a hand knit and a machine knit garment. This changed the way many Fair Isle textiles were made and led to machine knitting becoming part of Shetland's rich textile history.

My mom made sweaters with bands of Fair Isle at the yoke and cuff for me and my sister.

PART 2:
FAIR ISLE STYLE

SHETLAND WOOL

Shetland has been home to a unique breed of native sheep for centuries. There is evidence that primitive sheep have been in Shetland since Neolithic times. Later, the Vikings who settled and farmed here also brought sheep, adding to the number. These age-old sheep breeds have evolved into the native Shetland sheep we have today. Pure Shetland sheep are small animals, with characteristics that include short tails and soft, fine fleeces of many colors. The fleeces can be plucked or rooed (as it is said in Shetland).

Shetland sheep are a self-sufficient breed with a unique coat of wool, affording the animals great warmth during the high winds and endless rain typical of a harsh Shetland winter. They are hardy animals while still being nimble and light, ideally suited to the terrain in Shetland. They graze on heather and seaweed without the need for additional feed and are good mothers, being able to lamb themselves out in the hills entirely unaided. They are bred for both their meat and their fleece, their dense fleeces making a strong and versatile fiber once spun into a ball of yarn.

A Shetland sheep shows off its partially shed fleece.

There is crimp in this small hentilaget, which was left in the heather by a Shetland sheep as it sheds its own fleece.

I meet with a local crofter and the sheep that will produce Shetland wool.

Pure Shetland sheep tend to shed their fleece in the spring, so are often seen wandering around partially bald with long ribbons of fleece trailing behind them. These loose bits of fleece, which get caught in fences and in the heather, are known locally as hentilags or hentilagets. The growth of new fleece can cause a rise or weak point between the old and the new, allowing the old fleece to be plucked or rooed by hand. The rooed fleece, although labor intensive, can be among the softest because the fibers have no harsh cut ends, as can happen with a sheared fleece. Nowadays, most of the sheep are sheared much more efficiently using electric clippers.

The average staple length of Shetland fleece is around 3½" (8.9cm). The finest wool is around the neck and shoulders, with coarser wool on the hindlegs. The average diameter of fine wool is 10–20 microns while coarser wool averages 25–35 microns. One of the attributes a fleece grader is looking for is quality of the crimp, as there is a correlation between the fineness of the wool and crimp. Crimp is an important factor in providing the stretch, bounce, and shape recovery required for knitwear.

Living in Shetland, I find it satisfying to watch wool grow on the Shetland sheep, knowing that we will knit using that same locally grown wool the following winter. We will often know the crofter who breeds the sheep, the wool producers who process the wool, as well as the knowledgeable folk who sell the finished product. It is gratifying to trace the wool from local sheep to local wool shop.

Shetland wool is a remarkable natural fiber. It is naturally antibacterial due to its lanolin content. Shetland wool needs infrequent washing due to its self-cleaning properties, and for the most part, items can be hung out to air after wearing. It also has great insulating properties—warm in winter and cooler in the summer—a sensible and necessary choice for our climate in Shetland during both winter and summer.

The best results in Fair Isle knitting are achieved using 100% Shetland wool (2ply is equivalent to 4ply fingering weight). There are a few reasons for this:

1. Shetland wool has sticky qualities. By this, I mean that a strand of wool will naturally hook into the fibers around it and not unravel. This allows knitters to work in the round, steek, and cut their knitting without worrying about their work fraying. The strands at the back also hook into the main body of work, creating a dense fabric. It is difficult to create a traditional and attractive piece of Fair Isle knitting with a smoother or more slippery yarn.
2. There is a very large selection of colors available from our Shetland yarn producers. This means that the opportunities for color blending are endless due to the number of shades available. Many of the shades are subtle in their differences, allowing the knitter to essentially paint with wool.
3. Two-ply jumper weight is a fine wool, creating pieces with a close gauge. Fair Isle is best shown off when knitted in this small gauge, as stitch definition disappears and the motifs become well defined and clear cut. The same results will not be achieved with a chunkier yarn. Once Shetland wool has been washed and "dressed," the work becomes fabric-like.

This Fair Isle example shows off the small gauge stitch definition achieved with Shetland wool.

ALTERNATIVES TO SHETLAND WOOL

Other wools should be compatible with Fair Isle, as the 2ply jumper weight of Shetland wool is equivalent to 4ply yarn. I would recommend using an alternative real wool. Synthetic yarns and cotton yarns are too slippery and fray when being cut (for steeks). The finish also would appear shiny and would not have the same look as a real-wool sweater. Fair Isle–inspired garments in synthetic yarns do exist, but they are, for the most part, machine knitted. A genuine Fair Isle garment is knitted in Shetland wool.

If using a yarn other than Shetland wool, please note that results can't be guaranteed to be the same, and that it might be more technically challenging to use with the techniques presented in this book. For example, I have knitted baby hats in merino wool, which worked fine, but I would be reluctant to attempt steeking and cutting this wool in a more complex knit (see page 44).

Each project lists the exact yarn brand and color that I used if you want to replicate the hat, gansey, or mitts exactly as shown. However, this is just for reference. Pick a wool yarn and a color palette that appeals to you.

SHETLAND YARN PRODUCERS

Shetland wool from trusted yarn producers is the perfect choice for hand knitting both Shetland lace and Fair Isle, as well as for knitwear manufacture and weaving. Below are some big names in the business. However, as the popularity of Shetland wool grows, it is rewarding to see many smaller 100% Shetland wool producers popping up: Aister 'oo,' Foula Wool, Langsoond Yarn, Laxdale Yarn, and West Lynne Wool to name a few.

Jamieson's of Shetland

Jamieson's is a family business specializing in wool from Shetland sheep. Their business started in the early 1890s when local crofters brought knitwear to be bought or exchanged for goods. The garments were then sold outside of Shetland to meet the public demand for fashionable Shetland knitwear.

In 1981, Jamieson's Spinning Mill was opened, Shetland's only commercial woolen mill producing Shetland yarn. This unique mill, in Sandness, Shetland, completes all the stages of yarn production under one roof. This includes grading, scouring, and dyeing fleece before color blending, carding, spinning, twisting, and balling to produce their 100% pure Shetland yarn. With the business now moving into its fifth generation, they continue to develop and promote Shetland wool and its finished products.

Jamieson & Smith

Jamieson & Smith (also known as The Wool Broker) started in the 1930s. It was founded by the Smith family of Berry Farm in Scalloway, Shetland. In the 1960s, they relocated to their current premises in Lerwick. Their buildings include wool sheds and the yarn shop, which was formerly an old church.

According to their website, "Jamieson & Smith Shetland Wool Brokers Ltd. purchase Shetland wool from over 700 of Shetland's crofters and farmers, and transform it into high-quality Shetland wool products, including yarns, knitwear, blankets, and carpets." The fleeces are hand sorted and graded, ensuring that nothing is wasted. The coarser parts of the fleece are used in carpets and mats.

Jamieson & Smith aim to enhance the profile of Shetland wool, playing an important part in sustaining Shetland's wool industry.

Uradale Yarns

Uradale yarn comes from organically raised, native Shetland sheep. The sheep are naturally multicolored, so their undyed yarns reflect the natural colors of the flock. Uradale yarn is certified organically scoured, and then it is gently spun horizontally, resulting in a strong and even twine. Their dyed yarn is organically dyed, and both the shades and color names are based on the plants that grow around Uradale. Their yarn is unbleached, meaning that more of the natural lanolin is retained in the wool. This makes the yarn soft, strong, insulating, and water repellent.

Shetland sheep will climb on the cliffs of the Shetland Islands.

MURRISTER WIRSET

Shetland wool is without doubt a special product; hence, I became fascinated in completing the process from fleece to finished ball of yarn. This has led me to start my own small venture, called Murrister Wirset, in partnership with local crofter Hubert Moar. Hubert produces top-quality Shetland sheep and focuses on the welfare of the animal. Generations of good sheep breeding and management has led to sheep with high-quality fleece. We decided to develop our own small batch of Shetland wirset (yarn) together, using the best of his top-grade fleeces. As of the printing of this book, Murrister Wirset is in the early stages of development, but I hope to expand this project in the near future.

After Shetland sheep are clipped, the fleeces are sorted, skirted, and cleaned before being turned into wool.

I'm excited to present my own brand of Shetland wool yarn.

In my stash of Shetland wool from Jamieson's, Jamieson & Smith, and Uradale, I sort the balls by light and dark colors.

YARN QUANTITIES

Yarn quantity is one of the most difficult aspects to gauge. However, from my experience for an average-sized woman's gansey, around (18–20) 25g balls are required. More balls would be necessary for larger sizes, and quantities would also depend on the number of colours used. (Use 100% Shetland wool, but note that 2ply is equivalent to a 4ply or fingering weight.) Within the total amount, it is always difficult to gauge how much of each color.

One way to more accurately estimate the yarn quantity needed is to make a decent-sized swatch. Once a swatch has been knitted, weigh the remainder of the ball of each shade used, the difference between the starting and finishing weight being the amount of wool used. From there, multiply the number of similar-sized swatches that will be needed to complete the finished project.

A hat weighs approximately 50 grams, so a minimum of (2) 25g balls would be required for plain knitting; however, when using multiple colors for Fair Isle, at least one ball of each additional color is needed.

Also bear in mind that more wool will be used in Fair Isle knitting than in plain knitting due to the nature of carrying strands at the back of the work, causing the fabric to be double thickness.

Colors may vary between batches and are not always consistent if you need to order more later. This applies to both the natural and dyed shades. Therefore, it is best to err on the side of caution and overestimate yarn quantities when making a purchase. The remaining wool can easily be used on other smaller Fair Isle projects.

PATTERNS

Traditional Fair Isle motifs follow these general rules:

- **Use no more than a few consecutive stitches of any one color.** This is to avoid long strands of the second color at the back.
- **Most of the spaces are decorated.** Avoid large expanses without design.
- **Use two contrasting strands of wool at a time on each round.** Three is not usually used. This means that the work becomes a double-thickness fabric, which is beneficial for insulation and warmth. This is, of course, what Shetland wool is renowned for. It also means that the finished piece is seamless.

There are hundreds of Fair Isle motifs to choose from, and they are now well documented in many publications. Here is a collection of the most common patterns.

ROW PATTERNS

Common motifs are the 3-, 4-, or 5-row border patterns; the 7-, 9-, or 11-row peerie patterns; and the 15- or 17-row larger patterns. It includes the OXO motifs already mentioned. These are usually simplified geometric shapes, most often using diagonal lines, zigzags, diamonds, and crosses. Rounded shapes are less easy to achieve. These patterns are knitted in horizontal bands, joining to keep the pattern continuous in the round.

Umsket Gansey (page 140) shows motifs knitted in horizontal bands.

Large star patterns of about 25 rows are often used for gloves on the back of the hand.

Large star patterns are also used in traditional yoke sweaters.

ALLOVER PATTERNS

There are the "allover" patterns that join both horizontally and vertically to decorate the entire garment.

PEERIE PATTERNS

Traditionally, peerie patterns are alternated with larger patterns in a horizontal design. Patterns should sit on top of each other for symmetry and organization, and they should be centered at the front of the gansey.

VERTICAL PATTERNS

Motifs can also be arranged in vertical panels, often using seed stitch patterns as fillers between the vertical motifs, under the arms, and down the sides.

My daughter Nina hand knitted this allover gansey by herself.

The Virdik Vest (page 132) shows motifs sitting on top of each other in a uniform way.

One of my designs, the "Stovenswala Gansey," with vertical panel motifs on a traditional blocking frame (or jumper board).

GRAPH BOOKS

In most rural Shetland homes, even today, there will be a notebook of graph paper, hand drawn in dots with our traditional heritage. These books offer a range of motifs to choose from when starting a project. They are often passed down through many generations. It is now possible to purchase charts of our heritage motifs in a variety of modern publications.

My mother's graph book with motifs hand dotted in pen. The motifs sketched in her book were passed down from her mother.

COLORS

With so many color choices available in Shetland wool, it is a relatively easy job to find colors that blend. The more challenging bit is to blend both background and foreground, ensuring that there is enough contrast. The pattern needs to stand out against the background to ensure the Fair Isle motif does not disappear. Here are some tips for how to use color successfully:

- **Use contrasting colors.** I have chosen several shades for the contrasting colors, keeping them all quite dark, and several shades for the main colors, keeping them all quite light. Colors can be used vice versa too. This ensures that there is sufficient contrast for the motifs to show up.
- **Keep color changes subtle.** Notice that each of the shades (within the main colors or contrasting colors) blend from one into the next, so the color changes are subtle and hardly noticeable. The bold-stripe-look of clashing colors without harmony is to be avoided.
- **Experiment with color changes.** Designs that incorporate many color changes increase the complexity and richness of the design—but remember that only two colors are ever worked together on any given round.
- **Alternate main and contrasting colors.** Designs with horizontal bands of alternating patterns often switch main color and contrasting color between patterns. For example, a pattern might start with light foreground on a dark background and then be reversed in the next horizontal band.

Notice how I'm sorting my yarn by light and dark colors for the main and contrasting colors.

A highly contrasting color (red) is used in the center round of the main motif.

Umsket Gansey (page 140) shows how the main color (background) has changed from dark to light using progressive, gradual shading in the diamonds. From there, the dark colors have been used on the light background and some complementary contrasting colors have been used to brighten the dark background.

- **Use an accent color.** Although Shetland knitting is very much about keeping color changes subtle, a line of contrasting color is often used at the center row of the design. This often seems to lift the design, bringing an otherwise flat piece of work to life.
- **Know when to change colors.** Avoid changing both background and foreground colors at the same time, as that tends to make the design look as if it has been cut into segments. Better blending of color is achieved by changing them at least one round apart.
- **Make swatches.** Before knitting a large item, such as a gansey, practice with colors by knitting a few sample swatches to ensure you have chosen the correct color palette.
- **Compare strands for contrast.** When you are choosing yarns, a good way to check that there is enough contrast between two shades is to twist the two strands together. The two strands will merge if the shades are too alike to be used as contrasting colors.
- **Use natural light.** Always choose your shades for Fair Isle knitting in natural daylight. Colors can look quite different in artificial light.

There is enough contrast between these colors for one to be the main color and the other to be the contrasting color.

There isn't enough contrast here for a main color and contrasting color. These two shades would be better used to blend from one to the other on the background or foreground.

PART 3:
KNITTING HOW TO

EQUIPMENT

- **Boarding or Blocking Equipment**—See Washing and Dressing (page 48).
- **Double-Pointed Needles** (**DPNs**)—Or use your preferred needles. DPNs are for working circumferences in the round. In Shetland, it is traditional to knit with three double-pointed needles. The total number of stitches is normally divided between two needles, so that there is a front and a back needle and a third working needle.
- **Knitting Belt** (**Optional**)—See opposite page.
- **Measuring Tape**—Used to check tension and ensure your work is shaping up to be the right size. A small retractable one is ideal.
- **Scissors**—Good, sharp ones are ideal for cutting steeks.
- **Stitch Holders**—These are useful to hold live stitches that will be picked up again later; for example, when dropping underarm or neck stitches.
- **Stitch Markers**—They are sometimes used to mark the central stitch at the front or to place a mark at the side to distinguish between front and back (this is more common when using circular needles). In Shetland, knitters are more likely to use a scrap of waste yarn to place a marker.
- **Tapestry Needle**—I am quite fussy about which tapestry needle I use and have a favorite. It needs to be medium-sized but with a large enough eye to accommodate two strands of yarn when weaving in ends. It also needs to be blunt, as a sharp one will split the wool.

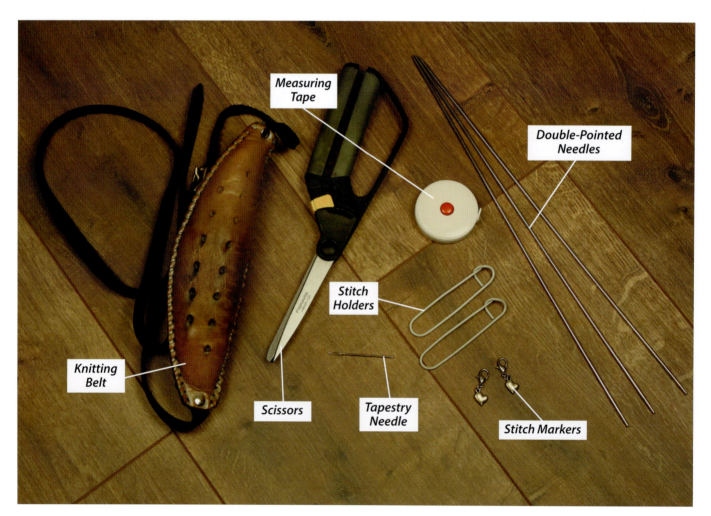

KNITTING BELT

A knitting belt (known locally as a makkin belt) is a leather pad, traditionally stuffed with horsehair. It's worn around the waist with the pad on the right-hand side. The right-hand needle is stuck into one of the holes in the pad; this gives the needle rigidity, keeps the knitting secure, sustains an even tension, and allows the knitter to work at speed. Knitting with a belt also frees up the right hand for holding yarns, and its use significantly decreases strain on shoulders, arms, and wrists.

In the past, knitting belts were worn all day to enable the knitter to pick up and drop their knitting easily as they went about their household tasks, with the main body of the knitting being tucked into the belt. Women could not afford to waste valuable time not knitting. Knitting was done as they walked to the hills to gather peat for fuel and on the way back again with heavy kishies full of peat on their backs.

I will wear a knitting belt when creating a Fair Isle project.

My great-grandmother Annie and her sister Mary carrying peats from the hill to their home. Annie (on the left) is knitting with a makkin belt as she walks.

KNITTING IN THE ROUND

Hand-knitted Fair Isle is always circular and knitted in the round. This is typically achieved by knitting with three double-pointed needles. The total number of stitches is halved, having front stitches on one needle, back stitches on a second needle, and using a third working needle. Sometimes four needles must be used in a bigger garment with large numbers of stitches.

There are two main factors to consider when knitting in the round.

DESIGN

Probably the most important factor in knitting in the round is to choose motifs that fit into the round of the total stitch number. In fact, the final number of stitches is usually determined by the chosen motifs and the stitch count is adjusted to ensure the repeats fit into the round. To my mind, it is a Shetland makkin crime if the motifs do not join and meet up in the round!

TIP

Holding a mirror along the halfway point of a motif in your knitting will enable you to visualize the design as a whole and give you an idea whether your choice of colors is working.

Notice the continuity of pattern at the shoulder join.

Traditionally, Shetland knitting is all about symmetry. If an imaginary line were drawn down the center front, there would be symmetry to either side of that line. The motifs themselves are repeated, creating a uniform look. As well as this, each motif is knitted up to the middle row and the second half is knitted as a mirror image of the first half. In the sleeves, the order of the motifs knitted in the body are knitted in reverse from the top down.

The shoulders are joined using either the three-needle cast-off method or by grafting the back and front shoulder stitches together. How the pattern will meet at the shoulders needs to be thought about in the planning stage. It is important that the pattern meets in a pleasing way at the shoulder, with either the two outer edges of the pattern meeting or the centers of the motif meeting, so that half the motif is on the back and half is on the front.

STRUCTURE

Knitting in the round means that knit stitches are used throughout. This is because it is much easier to knit Fair Isle on the outward side of the work, thus being able to see the pattern emerge, as opposed to maintaining the pattern while purling on the reverse side. Purl stitches are not used, apart from the ribbing. Hats, scarves, gloves, socks, and ganseys are all knitted this way: starting off as a tube, and then being shaped further on in the design as necessary.

Shetland ganseys are knitted straight to the underarms. Underarm stitches are then dropped and added to stitch holders. To continue knitting in the round and maintain that tubular shape, extra stitches are then cast on to close the armhole and neck openings. This enables continued knitting in the round to the shoulders. These extra stitches are known as "steek" stitches—not a traditional word in Shetland, but one that we have all now adopted.

Inevitably, there will be a slight jog in colorwork knitting where one round ends and the next one starts. This occurs in highly patterned areas, more so than if the last stitch and first stitch are of the same color. This is why the round is started at the left-hand side in a gansey, as it is a less visible area. As most Shetland knitting is done in lightweight yarn and on relatively small needles, the jog is minimal at such a small gauge. Once the item has been washed and dressed, any jogs will become almost invisible.

There is an almost invisible left-hand side join where one round ends and another starts.

TIP

Once your knitting is a few inches long, tie a length of yarn horizontally around the body of your work, just under the knitting needles. This technique is useful if you have hundreds of stitches on double-pointed needles, as it holds your work together and stops stitches from coming off the ends of the needles. This band of yarn can be moved up the garment as you progress.

TENSION

It is important to maintain an even tension throughout the garment. This ensures that the work does not have areas of large, loose stitches that look like ladders or areas where the float at the back is so tight that the work puckers. This takes practice, but a rhythm will soon be found. To help with tension, hold yarns in a consistent way, whichever is your preferred method.

Floats should lie flat at the back of the work with just the right amount of slack. I constantly pull the knitted stitches on the right-hand needle toward me, smoothing and spreading them out as I go to ensure that the float is neither too loose nor too tight. It is advisable not to leave long floats at the back of the work if knitting a stretch in one color (see Catching Floats on page 39). Knitting with a makkin belt can assist the process, as I believe it helps to produce knitting that is more machine-like.

Measuring tension in a 4" x 4" (10 x 10cm) *square gives you a gauge.*

Get to know your own tension. Knit a swatch using two colors, wash and dry it, and work out how many stitches you knit per 4" (10cm). My tension is around 32 stitches and 38 rounds in 4" x 4" (10 x 10cm) using 2ply jumper-weight 100% Shetland wool on US 2.5 (3mm) knitting needles. Once your own personal tension has been worked out, you can decide how many stitches are required for the size you want by multiplying 4" x 4" (10 x 10cm) squares.

If you are knitting a pattern from a designer and you want to replicate the exact size, you should check your tension carefully, as everyone's tension is different. The easiest way to match the required tension is to adjust the needle size. Increasing or decreasing your needle size by 0.5mm can have a dramatic effect on the finished size.

> ## TIP
> To keep an even tension, pull a couple of yards of yarn away from the ball as you knit, so your yarns are always loose. If your yarn is knitted taut and pulled tight from the ball, your tension will deteriorate.

HOLDING YARN

There is, of course, more than one way to hold yarn, and it is important that you hold the yarn in a way that is comfortable for you. Generally, the most common way in Shetland is to hold both strands in the right hand: one yarn looped over the forefinger, and the other yarn over the middle finger.

It would be traditional to hold the main color on the index finger and the contrast color on the middle finger. In my family, the reason for this is said to be that the stitches made using the middle finger will be slightly looser than the ones made by the index finger. Therefore, this method ensures that the contrast color (or motif stitches) will stand out.

Others prefer the Continental way of knitting: a strand on each index finger or sometimes both strands in the left hand. Choose the way that feels most natural to you and keep it consistent.

The common Shetland way to hold yarn: one yarn looped over the forefinger and the other yarn over the middle finger of the right hand.

Both yarns are anchored between the ring and little finger, feeding the yarns through to the fore and middle finger.

TIP

Inevitably, your yarns will get tangled at some stage of the process. To untangle, hold the two balls of yarn up, letting the knitted piece dangle and untwist with gravity.

TECHNIQUES

CASTING ON/LAYING ON

There are several ways to cast on, but a common way in Shetland is the long-tail method using your thumb. The length of yarn needed will vary for different needle sizes and wool thicknesses, but about 8" (20cm) of yarn is needed for every 20 stitches.

TIP

When casting on in large numbers, it can be helpful to add a scrap of colored yarn every 50 stitches to help keep count. The scraps can simply be pulled out after the first couple of rounds once the correct number of stitches has been established.

In Shetland, the first row is known as the sweerie geng. The word "sweerie" stems from the Norse word "svår," meaning difficult. The word "geng" stems from the word "gång," meaning path or a way.

1.

Roughly measure the amount of yarn needed. Cast on the first stitch in the same way as a slip knot.

2.

For the next stitch, wrap the yarn around your thumb from front to back in a clockwise direction.

3.

Knit into it, using yarn from the ball, as if your thumb was a knitting needle.

4.

Get into a rhythm, even if it is a slow one, to maintain even tension. Continue in this way until the required number of stitches has been cast on.

After casting on the required number of stitches along one needle, join the work to knit in the round by putting half the stitches on one needle and the other half on the second needle (if working with long double-pointed needles). Be careful not to twist your work.

When getting started, the first round is always the hardest round to knit, as it is tricky knitting into cast-on stitches that have not been knitted before. It is best to take this round slowly because it is easy to lose a stitch, and this inevitably means starting from scratch again.

RIBBING

Ribbing can be made in one color, often the main color, and this is called **single-color ribbing**. Alternatively, it can be made in more than one color when the knit stitches are made in one shade (or set of shades) and the purl stitches are made in contrasting shades (or set of shades). This is called **corrugated ribbing**.

Single-color ribbing has more bounce and stretch than corrugated ribbing, which is restricted with strands floating at the back. As a result, fewer stitches are required for single-color ribbing. Corrugated ribbing makes for an interesting start to a garment, as the colors that you plan to use in the design can be introduced in either the knit or purl stitches. With either type, the stitch count must then be increased for the Fair Isle part of the garment, which keeps the ribbing tight and springy, leaving the main body of colorwork looser.

Corrugated ribbing is most often done in knit two, purl two; however, there are sometimes variations on this, such as knit one, purl one. The main color can be worked on either the knit stitches or the purl stitches, and the contrast color on the other. There are advantages with both ways.

Neck examples of single-color ribbing (top) and corrugated ribbing (bottom).

Contrasting color is used in the purl stitches (top). Contrasting color is used in the knit stitches (bottom). Both show blending to the center of the ribbing, which is then reversed on the second half.

- If the main color (MC) used for the cast on is used for the knit stitches and the contrast color (CC) is used for the purl stitches, purl bumps become visible on the first round of introducing a color. To avoid purl bumps, my method is to use knit stitches in both the MC and CC in the first round, and then commence purl stitches in the CC on the second round. The purl bumps do not matter so much with subsequent color changes in the purl stitches, especially if color blending is subtle. Indeed, those rounds can be viewed as a useful graduation between the colors.

- If the CC is introduced on the knit stitches and the MC used for the cast on is used for the purl stitches, these purl bumps do not happen. This can be an advantage, but it does mean that color changes in the knit stitches can look abrupt and lacking in subtlety.

It is very much knitter's preference, and I do both. If I had to choose, I prefer seeing my knit stitches in the main color and my purl stitches in the contrasting color, so most of the designs in this book start with "knit two MC, knit two CC" in the first round.

INCREASING

There are several ways to increase the number of stitches in the round, and which way chosen depends on the knitter's preference and the context of where the increases are to be placed. Here are some methods I prefer.

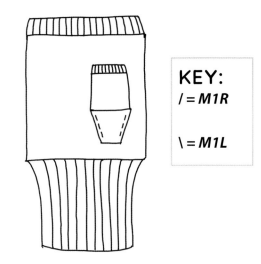

In a general increase round where the number of stitches is being increased (for example, between the ribbing and the colorwork section), the increases will always be done on a plain round without pattern. The method I use is to knit into the front and then knit into the back of the same stitch before taking it off the left-hand needle (KFB). This is an easy method to do, leaving a small bar across the front of the knitting. But because it is on a plain color round, it is hardly noticeable.

When increasing in a thumb gusset on a pair of gloves or mitts, it is preferable for those increases to be less visible and without the small bar. For these, I would use right- and left-leaning increases.

- **Make one to the right (M1R)**—Lift the bar between stitches from back to front, and knit through the front of this loop. This creates a right-leaning stitch increase that is in keeping with the shape of the right side of the thumb gusset.
- **Make one to the left (M1L)**—Lift the bar between stitches from front to back, and knit through the back of this loop. This creates a left-leaning stitch increase that is in keeping with the shape of the left side of the thumb gusset.

DECREASING

In a general decrease round where the number of stitches is being decreased (for example, after the colorwork section in preparation for the crown of a hat), the decreases will also always be done on a plain round without pattern. The usual way here is to knit two stitches together (K2tog)—as if they were one stitch—at regular intervals all the way around.

In colorwork sections (for example, at the sides of the armholes or the sides of the neck), it is preferred that these decreases look more symmetrical. Knit two together is a right-leaning decrease that slants the stitches to the right. This is perfect for right-slanting decrease lines. Another method to reduce two stitches into one is to slip one stitch, knit the next stitch, then pass the slipped stitch over the knitted stitch (SKP). This method creates left-leaning decreases.

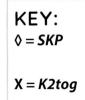

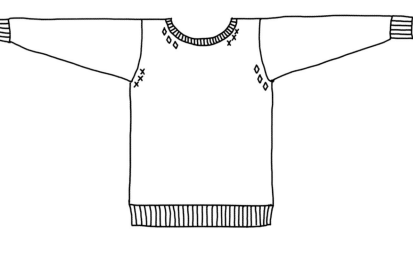

JOINING YARNS

Color changes are always done at the start of the round, and the ends are woven in later. However, if it is necessary to join yarns in the middle of the round, the best method I have found is as follows:

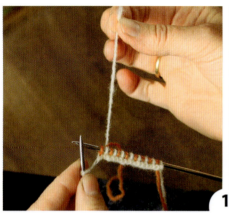

With the last 4" (10cm) of yarn, create a loop.

1.

Twist the two sides of the loop strands together. Knit the next couple of stitches using the double strands.

2.

Once the end of the loop has been secured, take the new yarn and thread it through the loop.

3.

Fold the new yarn back on itself, creating a second loop like a chain.

4.

Pull the new yarn taut, holding the end in place. Continue to knit using the double-thickness strands until they are used up. Carry on knitting as usual with the new joined yarn.

5.

CATCHING FLOATS

When knitting with two colors, one of the colors is carried along at the back of the work. The name for these strands of yarn is "floats." If the float being carried at the back gets too long, it creates a loop that can get caught in fingers or snagged in jewelry. Most Fair Isle motifs are designed to have short floats, commonly around three to six stitches of one color, but there are some cases where the float is longer, and it needs to be caught and anchored to your fabric.

Seen here are short floats on the reverse side of a project.

> ### TIP
> If using Shetland yarn, the floats can be a little longer than when using a more slippery wool due to the sticky qualities of the fiber. The wool in the float naturally hooks into the wool on the main body of work after washing and dressing.

Catching floats is more likely to be needed in your main color (background), as this is where it is more likely to have long stretches of one color only. So, for example, if I had a background color stretch of nine stitches, I would catch the float on the fifth stitch.

How to Catch Floats

Assuming the main color (gray in this example) is held in front of your contrast color, catch the floats as follows:

1.

Insert the right-hand needle into the stitch as normal.

2.

Wrap the contrast color (red) around the front of the needle from front to back. This is the opposite way to a normal knit stitch.

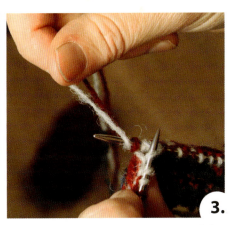

3.

Wrap the main color (gray) around the needle as if to knit as well.

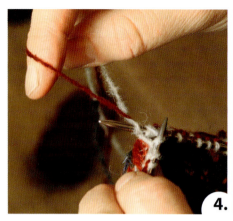

4. Unwrap the contrast color, taking it off again so that the main color is the only one left on the needle.

5. Continue to knit the stitch as normal in the main color. The contrast color then becomes caught under the main working yarn.

For long stretches of contrast color (blue in this example), catch the floats in a similar way, as follows:

1. Insert the right-hand needle into the stitch as normal.

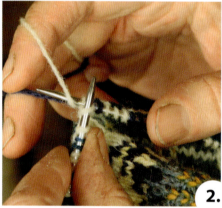

2. Wrap the main color (white) around the needle as if to knit.

3. Wrap the contrast color (blue) around the needle as if to knit as well.

4. Unwrap the main color, taking it off again so that the contrast color is the only one left on the needle.

5. Continue to knit the stitch as normal in the contrast color. The main color then becomes caught under the contrast yarn.

CASTING OFF

Casting off is usually done after a section of ribbing. After single-color ribbing, it is important to cast off loosely. The ribbing is then usually folded over, such as in a hat brim. In a round-neck gansey, it is cast off, folded over, and stitched down.

For corrugated ribbing where the edge will be on show, casting off is done neatly in ribbing, using the main color only. It would not be usual practice to fold over a corrugated ribbing, as the result would be too bulky.

1.

Knit one, pass the previous stitch over.

2.

Purl one, pass the previous stitch over.

3.

There should never be more than two stitches on the right-hand needle at one time. The top edge should look neat and even, neither too slack nor too tight.

It's fairly common to see sheep wandering in search of food. Even on the roads!

For joining two edges, such as the shoulder seam, the traditional way would be grafting (also known as Kitchener stitch). The same results can be achieved using a three-needle cast off. Both techniques are described here.

Grafting

Leave a long piece of yarn on one half for grafting. Otherwise, thread a tapestry needle with the required length of yarn to close the seam (often the main color). Take the two edges to be joined and hold the knitting needles together parallel in your left hand, with the right side of the work outermost. Steps 1 and 2 are preparatory, ensuring the yarn is in the correct starting position.

Insert the tapestry needle purlwise into the first stitch on the front needle. Pull the yarn through, leaving the stitch on the knitting needle.

1.

Insert the tapestry needle knitwise into the first stitch on the back needle. Pull the yarn through, leaving the stitch on the knitting needle.

2.

3.

Insert the tapestry needle knitwise into the first stitch on the front needle. Slip the stitch off the knitting needle.

4.

Insert the tapestry needle purlwise into the next stitch on the front needle. Pull the yarn through, leaving the stitch on the knitting needle.

5.

Insert the tapestry needle purlwise into the first stitch on the back needle. Slip the stitch off the needle.

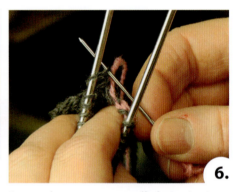

6.

Insert the tapestry needle knitwise into the next stitch on the back needle. Pull the yarn through, leaving the stitch on the knitting needle.

7.

Repeat steps 3–6 until all the stitches are used up, keeping an even tension with the yarn on the tapestry needle. Do not pull too tight.

8.

Once finished, the two pieces are grafted together with a row of stockinette stitches that looks the same as a knitted row. An invisible join would be achieved using yarn of the same color as the knitted item.

Three-Needle Cast Off

1. *Turn the work inside out, so that the right sides are facing each other. Take the two edges to be joined and hold them together parallel in your left hand.*

2. *Insert the right-hand knitting needle through the first stitch of the front needle and then the first stitch of the back needle, knitting them together.*

3. *Repeat step 2 on the second stitch on both needles.*

4. *Once there are two stitches on the right-hand needle, pass the first stitch over the second stitch.*

5. *Repeat steps 2–4. There should never be more than two stitches on the right-hand needle at one time.*

6. *The finished join looks like a chain of stitches on the inside.*

7. *If using a closing yarn of the same color, the two edges would have a neat and invisible join on the outside.*

STEEKING

On the Virdik Vest (page 132), the steeks look like a grouping of horizontal lines that break up the consistent pattern seen elsewhere.

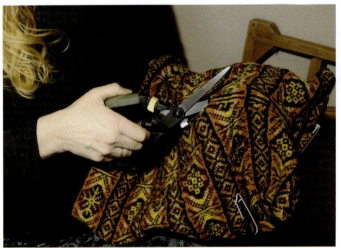

Cut into the steek stitches to create an opening; here, it's for the neck.

When cutting steek stitches, place your free hand at the back of the scissors. This prevents accidently cutting through both layers of fabric.

Steek stitches are extra stitches that are cast on to form a bridge, allowing the garment to be knitted in the round. Later, steek stitches are cut to create openings for armholes, the neck, or the center front. Steeks are knitted in what is known in Shetland as "one and one," meaning one stitch is knitted in the main color, the next stitch is knitted in the contrast color, and then this is repeated. This ensures that both colors are carried across the steek stitches to start the next patterned area. The two outermost steek stitches should always be in the main color, so that they blend into the main body of work.

Knitting steeks in columns also ensures that there are straight lines of color to follow when cutting steeks open. Steek stitches are cut before adding the neck and sleeves. Once the steek is opened, the edges will naturally curl under. The edges can be stitched down at this point, but I usually pick up stitches and knit the neck or sleeves first, leaving the steek to be stitched down afterward.

At the armhole edge, the start of the round should start in the middle of the steek at the underarm. For example, if eight steek stitches have been cast on, it would be normal Shetland practice to move four stitches to each double-pointed needle, so that the round starts in the middle of the steek. When the steek is cut, all the joining yarns will fall off rather than having to be woven in.

Stitches are picked up from the bar between the last steek stitch and the first stitch from the main body of work.

← NEEDLE

Sketch shows picking up the bars between the columns of stitches.

Sleeve and Neck Edge

Examples of this would be when picking up stitches at the armhole to knit the sleeve from the top downward or around the neck to make the neckband. It is tempting to pick up the right leg of a knitted stitch, but as this stitch stretches, this method can lead to large loops and gaps between the armhole and sleeve.

- **Method 1:** A common Shetland method is to look for the bar between two columns of stitches, picking up one bar at a time, and knitting it with the main color. When picking up from an edge with a steek, pick up and knit from the bar between the outermost steek stitch and the first edge stitch of the main body of work.
- **Method 2:** Alternatively, pick up the right leg of the edge stitch along with the left leg of the outermost steek stitch. Knit the two legs together with the main color.

Whichever way the stitches are picked up, make sure it is done with a very thin knitting needle, as this is much easier than using a chunkier one. I use a US 0 (2mm) needle to pick up stitches.

With both methods, it is best to pick up a stitch for every row knitted and then reduce the number of stitches to the correct amount on the next round. This avoids gaps that otherwise might occur by attempting to pick up the correct number on the first round.

ALTERNATIVE TO STEEKING

Some Shetlanders do not steek but prefer to *brak an eke*, as it is believed that this method can be less bulky. This is when the knitter breaks the yarns off at the end of each row. The yarns are then rejoined at the start to work another right-side row.

This brak an eke technique is used in the brim of the Sukkaburdie Bonnet (page 94).

Around the Thumb of a Glove

Stitches around the thumb of a glove are picked up on both sides of the waste yarn that has been knitted in to mark the opening. This piece of waste yarn is best as a highly contrasting color, so it is easier to see when removed.

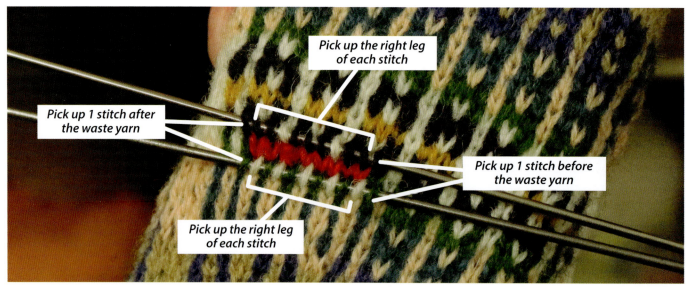

The stitches have been picked up around the waste yarn (shown in red) at the thumb for these mitts.

Pick up the right leg of each stitch. In addition, pick up one stitch just before the waste yarn, followed by one more after the waste yarn on both sides (four extra stitches total). This ensures neat corners and avoids gaps at either side of the thumb. Using this method, there will be more stitches than required, but the number can be adjusted on the next round.

Alternate using a tapestry needle and scissors to pull and snip the waste thread.

Once the waste yarn is removed, a thumb opening is left for the glove or mitt.

Once the live stitches are safely on the needles, the waste yarn can be snipped out carefully. Pull one stitch with a tapestry needle, then use sharp scissors to cut, repeating as needed. The rest of the thumb can be knitted up in the round.

The starting point of the thumb is not crucial, but the traditional Shetland method is to start the first round at the inner side of the thumb nearest to the center of the palm. The reason behind this is to avoid the starting point on the outer edge of the thumb, which might look less neat.

FINISHING

Steek stitches are typically stitched down prior to picking up sleeve stitches. This method is described below. Alternatively, it is equally acceptable to pick up and knit both sleeves and neck first, leaving the steek stitches to be stitched down at the very end before washing and dressing. Steeks knitted in Shetland wool tend not to fray.

Stitch down the steeks.

Encourage the edges to roll under at either side. Hand sew the edges in place.

Make sure a sewing stitch is put into every knitted stitch to secure. Using Shetland wool, there is no need to reinforce the edges before cutting.

Tighten any knots and weave in the ends. I weave in both ends at a time.

Choose five or six taut floats at the back to weave into, rather than loose ones, to keep the ends neat. Some would choose to separate the two ends, weaving one end on one side and one end on the other side.

WASHING AND DRESSING

WASHING

Shetland wool should be carefully washed, as it tends to felt and shrink if not handled gently.

1. Wash in mild soap.
2. Leave to soak for a short while, rather than agitating the fibers aggressively in the water.
3. Rinse in two clean water rinses. Squeeze out the water by wrapping the item in a towel, or give it a very light spin in a washing machine.
4. The wool item then needs to be stretched/dressed.

Shetland wool is largely self-cleaning. It contains fatty acids that repel water as well as bacteria, allowing it to remain fresh after being worn. Avoid washing too often; instead, choose to hang your garment up to air between wears. Washing a gansey once or twice a year is sufficient. Over-washing will result in loss of the natural grease in the wool that keeps the fibers smooth and elastic. This would lead to shrinkage, pilling, and loss of shape of the garment.

DRESSING

Virdik Vest (page 132) on a blocking frame that is adjustable in size for both width and length.

If the garment has sleeves, adjustable struts are added from underarm to cuff to give the sleeves shape.

In Shetland, wooden boards are used to stretch all woolen items in a process that is known locally as "dressing." These boards are often made by family members and in the past would have been made from driftwood from the sea. Nowadays, it is possible to buy boarding equipment from many of the Shetland wool suppliers, or boards can be made from thin plywood.

Dressing is an important process. As well as stretching the garment, it flattens and evens out the stitches, fluffing up the fiber to become smooth and fabric-like. It also ensures that any curling of the ribbing disappears. Leave the garment on the board or blocking mat to dry.

Stretchers can also be made from thick cardboard. Lay your finished knitting on a piece of cardboard and draw the shape onto the cardboard about 1" (2.5cm) bigger all over (or to your preferred finished measurements). Cut the cardboard to shape, and cover it in plastic wrap to prevent the cardboard becoming soggy. Insert the stretcher inside your finished knitted piece and leave it to dry.

Hats are often stretched on upside-down pudding bowls, and berets can be stretched on small dinner plates.

Once dry, steam may be required to pull in the ribbing again, as those parts often become over-stretched. This can be done very carefully using steam from a kettle or a steam iron, although no actual pressure should be applied from the iron, as this will crush the wool fibers. Alternatively, just dampen the ribbing and pull it into shape.

It should be said that although Shetland wool needs gentle handling during the washing process, when it comes to the dressing process, the garment can be handled slightly more assertively and will come to no harm.

Sock, glove, mitten, scarf, and blocking frames in various sizes from child to adult.

Each pattern provides detailed instructions for how to make the project as well as the Shetland inspiration behind it. Color diagrams are included for your reference. Note: Even though I provided the yarn I used, you don't need to use the same brand or color to make your garment. Some alternative colorways are scattered throughout.

PART 4:
PATTERNS

HOW TO READ THE CHARTS

As you work on the projects in this book, stitch charts are used to accompany the text instructions. The instructions are written, and the Fair Isle work is charted.

Read all the charts from right to left using the colors suggested or colors of your choosing. Color charts are provided at the beginning of each project to indicate what yarn I used, and they serve as a key to the charts. The colors used are also listed in the columns on the right-hand side of the charts. The background color—or main color (MC)—is listed in the right column, and the foreground color—or contrast color (CC)—is in the left column.

The repeated sections are marked within a colored box. Red, green, and blue boxes are used throughout this book; the example on the opposite page shows green. Green lines indicate the stitches that will be picked up later for a thumb (on mitts or gloves).

If the pattern features multiple sizes in the directions, then multiple charts of the same section will be provided. There will be slight differences between the two to accommodate the slight variation in the pattern, so it's important that you follow only the chart in the size you are working.

Assume knit stitches are used unless otherwise noted. These notes will appear as symbols on the chart (such as a dot for purl or an X for K2tog). A key accompanies all charts for quick reference, but all symbols are explained on page 148.

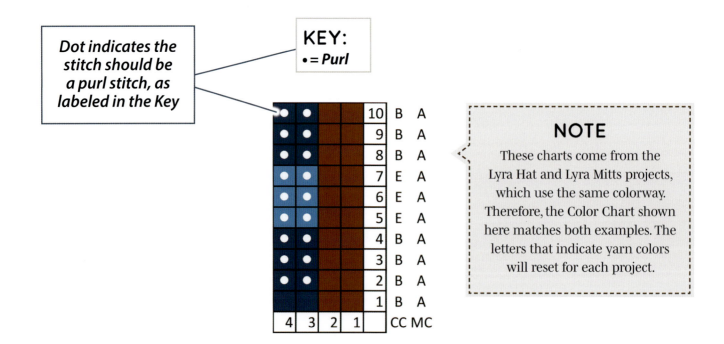

Dot indicates the stitch should be a purl stitch, as labeled in the Key

KEY:
• = Purl

NOTE

These charts come from the Lyra Hat and Lyra Mitts projects, which use the same colorway. Therefore, the Color Chart shown here matches both examples. The letters that indicate yarn colors will reset for each project.

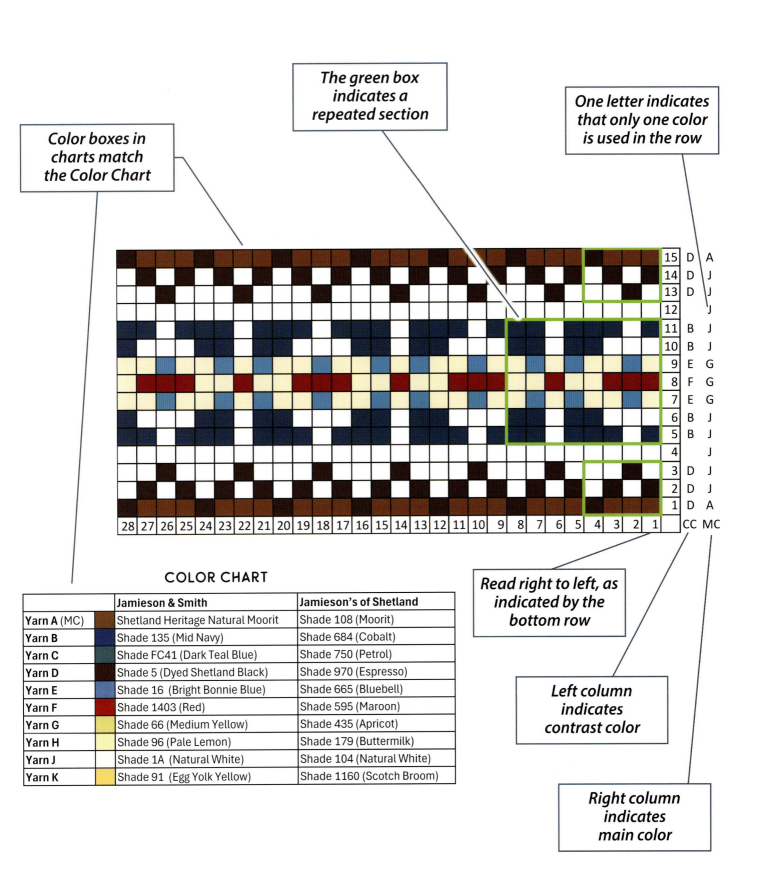

Color boxes in charts match the Color Chart

The green box indicates a repeated section

One letter indicates that only one color is used in the row

Read right to left, as indicated by the bottom row

Left column indicates contrast color

Right column indicates main color

COLOR CHART

		Jamieson & Smith	Jamieson's of Shetland
Yarn A (MC)		Shetland Heritage Natural Moorit	Shade 108 (Moorit)
Yarn B		Shade 135 (Mid Navy)	Shade 684 (Cobalt)
Yarn C		Shade FC41 (Dark Teal Blue)	Shade 750 (Petrol)
Yarn D		Shade 5 (Dyed Shetland Black)	Shade 970 (Espresso)
Yarn E		Shade 16 (Bright Bonnie Blue)	Shade 665 (Bluebell)
Yarn F		Shade 1403 (Red)	Shade 595 (Maroon)
Yarn G		Shade 66 (Medium Yellow)	Shade 435 (Apricot)
Yarn H		Shade 96 (Pale Lemon)	Shade 179 (Buttermilk)
Yarn J		Shade 1A (Natural White)	Shade 104 (Natural White)
Yarn K		Shade 91 (Egg Yolk Yellow)	Shade 1160 (Scotch Broom)

DAGA POKKI

Daga Pokki is a small and simple project to get you started if you are new to Fair Isle knitting. It is made in three colors only. The pouch can be used to hold small objects or as a phone case for an average-sized mobile phone. *Pokki* is the word we would use in Shetland for a pouch or a small bag. *Daga* is the old Norse word for "day." *Hana Daga*, meaning "the day dawns," is a poem written in Shetland dialect by the well-known Shetland poet T. A. Robertson, also known as Vagaland.

×××××
××

YARN

- Jamieson & Smith 2ply Jumper Weight, 100% Shetland wool in 114 yards (105m)/25g balls; or Jamieson's of Shetland Spindrift, 100% Shetland wool in 114 yards (105m)/25g balls.
- Yarns A, B, and C: 1 ball of each, listed in the color chart.

NEEDLES

- US 2.5 (3mm) double-pointed needles or preferred needles for working in the round. Adjust size if needed to obtain the correct tension.
- An extra needle will be needed for three-needle cast off if circular needles are used.

NOTIONS

- Stitch markers, tapestry needle.

TENSION

- 30 sts and 38 rounds to 4" x 4" (10 x 10cm), in stranded colorwork, after blocking. Please pay particular attention to the required tension and adjust needle size accordingly.

FINISHED MEASUREMENTS

- Length: 6¾" (17cm)
- Circumference: 8" (20cm)

PATTERN NOTES

- The purse is knitted from the top down, starting with a section of corrugated ribbing. Work all charts from right to left using the colors suggested or colors of your choosing.

××

COLOR CHART

		Jamieson & Smith	Jamieson's of Shetland
Yarn A (MC)	⬛	Shade 77 (Dyed Black)	Shade 999 (Black)
Yarn B	⬜	Shade 1A (Natural White)	Shade 104 (Natural White)
Yarn C	🟥	Shade 9113 (Dark Red)	Shade 587 (Madder)

INSTRUCTIONS

Using A (MC), cast on 48 sts, dividing sts over two (or more) needles to knit in the round, being careful not to twist your work. If using circular needles instead of DPNs, pm to mark the beginning of the round.

Corrugated Ribbing

Round 1: *K1A, K1B; repeat from * to end of round.
Rounds 2–9: *K1A, P1B; repeat from * to end of round.
Next Round: Knit to end of round.
Inc Round: Using A (MC), *K3, KFB; repeat from * to end of round. *60 sts*.

Body

Begin working from Round 1 of Chart A, working the 30-stitch chart twice in the round. Continue working from Chart A as set, changing colors where indicated, until all 53 rounds are complete.
Turn work inside out, with half the sts on one needle and half on another. Using a third needle, work a three-needle cast off with A (MC) across all sts.

Finishing

Weave in the ends. Hand wash in mild, soapy water. Wrap in a towel to remove excess water. Stretch on stiff cardboard covered in plastic wrap or pull to shape and dry on a flat surface.

CHART A

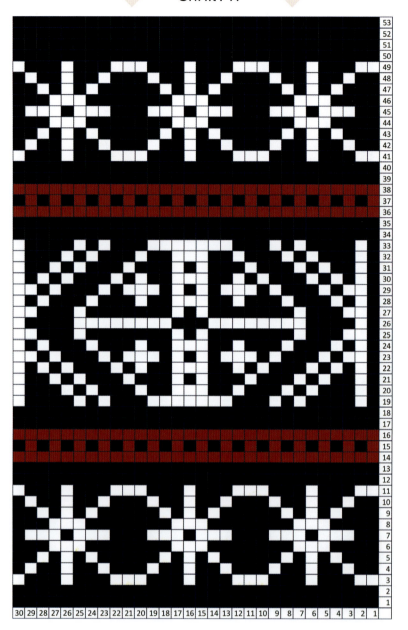

Although Shetland measures a mere approximately 50 miles (80km) long and 20 miles (32km) wide, it has a vast coastline of nearly 1,700 miles (2,736km) due to the complexity of the geology and the vast number of voes (bays), geos (gullies), inlets, and headlands. The word *hevda* features in a few place names in Shetland, stemming from the Norse word for a high and steep promontory of land, as seen throughout Shetlands landscape.

YARN

- Jamieson & Smith 2ply Jumper Weight, 100% Shetland wool in 114 yards (105m)/25g balls; or Jamieson's of Shetland Spindrift, 100% Shetland wool in 114 yards (105m)/25g balls.
- Yarns A, B, C, D, E, and F: 1 ball of each, listed on the color chart.

NEEDLES

- US 2.5 (3mm) double-pointed needles or preferred needles for working in the round. Adjust size if needed to obtain the correct tension.

NOTIONS

- Stitch markers, tapestry needle.

TENSION

- 30 sts and 38 rounds to 4" x 4" (10 x 10cm), in stranded colorwork, after blocking. Please pay particular attention to the required tension and adjust needle size accordingly.

FINISHED MEASUREMENTS

- Circumference (at brim): 20¼" (51cm)
- Length (from bottom to top): 4" (10cm)

PATTERN NOTES

- Work all charts from right to left using the colors suggested or colors of your choosing.

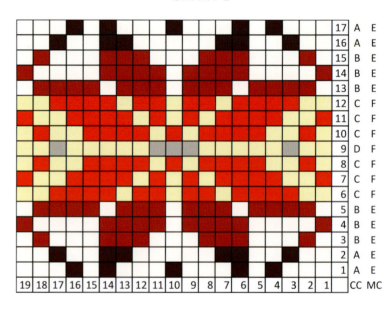

CHART A

	4	3	2	1		
2					D	E
1					D	A
	4	3	2	1		CC MC

CHART C

	4	3	2	1		
2					D	A
1					D	E
	4	3	2	1		CC MC

CHART B

17	A	E
16	A	E
15	B	E
14	B	E
13	B	E
12	C	F
11	C	F
10	C	F
9	D	F
8	C	F
7	C	F
6	C	F
5	B	E
4	B	E
3	B	E
2	A	E
1	A	E

Columns: 19 18 17 16 15 14 13 12 11 10 9 8 7 6 5 4 3 2 1 | CC MC

COLOR CHART

		Jamieson & Smith	Jamieson's of Shetland
Yarn A (MC)		Shade 2005 (Shetland Black)	Shade 101 (Shetland Black)
Yarn B		Shade 9113 (Dark Red)	Shade 587 (Madder)
Yarn C		Shade 1402 (Red)	Shade 525 (Crimson)
Yarn D		Shade 27 (Mid Grey)	Shade 320 (Steel)
Yarn E		Shade 1A (Natural White)	Shade 104 (Natural White)
Yarn F		Shade 96 (Pale Lemon)	Shade 179 (Buttermilk)

INSTRUCTIONS

Using A (MC), cast on 152 sts, and join to knit in the round, being careful not to twist your work. Pm to mark the beginning of the round.

Corrugated Ribbing

Round 1: *K2A, K2B; repeat from * to end of round.
Rounds 2–5: *K2A, P2B; repeat from * to end of round. Break off B.
Round 6: Continuing in A (MC), knit to end of round.
Inc Round 1: K4, *K8, KFB; repeat from * to last 4 sts, K4. *168 sts*.

Body

Work Rounds 1–2 of Chart A, repeating the four-stitch repeat 42 times around. At the end of Chart A, break off D.
Next Round: Continuing in E, knit to end of round.
Inc Round 2: *K55, KFB; repeat from * to end of round. *171 sts*.
Begin working from Round 1 of Chart B, working the 19-stitch repeat nine times around. Continue working from Chart B as set, changing colors where indicated, until all 17 rounds are complete.
Next Round: Using E, knit to end of round.
Dec Round 1: *K55, K2tog; repeat from * to end of round. *168 sts*.
Work Rounds 1–2 of Chart C, repeating the four-stitch repeat 42 times around. At the end of Chart C, break off D.
Next Round: Continuing with A (MC), knit to end of round.
Dec Round 2: K4, *K8, K2tog; repeat from * to last 4 sts, K4. *152 sts*.

Corrugated Ribbing

Round 1: *K2A, K2B; repeat from * to end of round.
Rounds 2–5: *K2A, P2B; repeat from * to end of round. Break off B.
Using A (MC), cast off neatly in K2, P2 rib pattern.

Finishing

Weave in the ends. Hand wash in mild, soapy water and rinse. Wrap in a towel to remove excess water or use a very light spin in a washing machine. Stretch over a pudding bowl of a suitable size and leave until dry. If the ribbing becomes too stretched, this can be pulled in again using steam if necessary.

TOOSIK BABY TOORIE

The Toosik Baby Toorie features a peerie 11-row pattern as the main motif. Zigzag color shading has been used effectively to take the background color from dark to light, and then from light to dark again for the crown. The crown design is an adaptation of a traditional Shetland crown.

Within Shetland, different words can vary between each district. *Toosik* is a Wastside word for "a small child who is slightly on the wild, unruly side." *Toorie* is the Shetland word for "a woolen hat."

×××××
××

YARN

- Jamieson's of Shetland Spindrift, 100% Shetland wool in 114 yards (105m)/25g balls.
- Yarns A, B, C, D, E, F, and G: 1 ball of each, listed in the color chart.

NEEDLES

- US 2.5 (3mm) double-pointed needles or preferred needles for working circumferences in the round. Adjust size if needed to obtain the correct tension.

NOTIONS

- Stitch markers, tapestry needle.

TENSION

- 30 sts and 38 rounds to 4" x 4" (10 x 10cm), in stranded colorwork, after blocking. Please pay particular attention to the required tension and adjust needle size accordingly.

FINISHED MEASUREMENTS

Small
- Circumference (at brim): 12½" (32cm)
- Circumference (at body): 13¾" (35cm)
- Length (from brim to crown): 5⅞" (15cm)

Medium
- Circumference (at brim): 13¾" (35cm)
- Circumference (at body): 15¼" (39cm)
- Length (from brim to crown): 5⅞" (15cm)

Large
- Circumference (at brim): 15¼" (39cm)
- Circumference (at body): 17⅛" (43.5cm)
- Length (from brim to crown): 6¾" (17cm)

PATTERN NOTES

- Read all charts from right to left using the colors suggested or colors of your choosing. Instructions are given for three sizes, represented by parentheses: Small (Medium, Large).

×××

COLOR CHART

		Jamieson's of Shetland
Yarn A (MC)		Shade 1340 (Cosmos)
Yarn B		Shade 127 (Pebble)
Yarn C		Shade 293 (Port Wine)
Yarn D		Shade 556 (Old Rose)
Yarn E		Shade 603 (Pot-Pourri)
Yarn F		Shade 104 (Natural White)
Yarn G		Shade 580 (Cherry)

INSTRUCTIONS

Using A (MC), cast on 92 (104, 116) sts, dividing sts over two needles to work in the round, being careful not to twist your work. If using circular needles, pm to mark the beginning of the round.

Small and Medium Only:

Begin working from Round 1 of Chart A, working the four-stitch repeat 23 (26) times in total around. Continue working from Chart A as set, changing colors where indicated, until all eight rounds are complete.

Break off B (CC) and continue with A (MC).

Round 9: Knit to end of round.

Inc Round: K6 (4), *K4 (5), KFB; repeat from * to last 6 (4) sts, K6. *108 (120) sts.*

Proceed to Body.

Large Only:

Begin working from Round 1 of Chart A, working the four-stitch repeat 29 times in total around. Continue working from Chart A as set, changing colors where indicated, until Round 5 is complete. Repeat Round 5 once more before proceeding with Rounds 6 8 (9 rounds worked in total).

Break off B (CC) and continue with A (MC).

Round 10: Knit to end of round.

Inc Round: K2, *K6, KFB; repeat from * to last 2 sts, K2. *132 sts.*

Proceed to Body.

Body

Begin working from Round 1 of Chart B, working the four-stitch repeat 27 (30, 33) times in total around. Continue working from Chart B as set, changing colors where indicated, until all nine rounds are complete. Break off D and continue in B.

Next Round (Inc Round): K0 (0, 2) *K26 (19, 15), KFB; repeat from * to end of round. *112 (126, 140) sts.*

Begin working from Round 1 of Chart C, working the 14-stitch repeat 8 (9, 10) times in total around. Continue working from Chart C as set, changing colors where indicated, until all 13 rounds are complete. Break off A (MC) and continue with B.

Next Round (Dec Round): K0 (0, 2) *K26 (19, 15), K2tog; repeat from * to end of round. *108 (120, 132) sts.*

Begin working from Round 1 of Chart D, working the four-stitch repeat 27 (30, 33) times in total around. Continue working from Chart D as set, changing colors where indicated, until all nine rounds are complete. Break off C and continue with A (MC).

Next Round (Dec Round): *K7 (13, 31), K2tog; repeat from * to end of round. *96 (112, 128) sts.*

CHART A

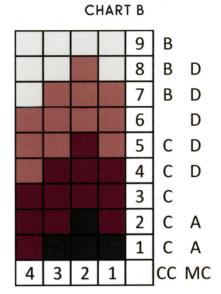

						CC	MC
●	●			8		B	A
●	●			7		B	A
●	●			6		B	A
●	●			5		E	A
●	●			4		E	A
●	●			3		B	A
●	●			2		B	A
				1		B	A
4	3	2	1			CC	MC

CHART B

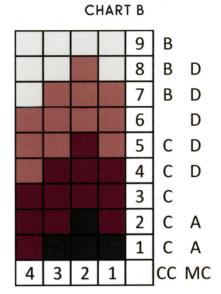

				9	B	
				8	B	D
				7	B	D
				6		D
				5	C	D
				4	C	D
				3	C	
				2	C	A
				1	C	A
4	3	2	1		CC	MC

CHART C

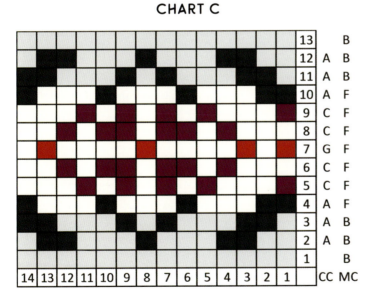

Row	CC	MC
13		B
12	A	B
11	A	B
10	A	F
9	C	F
8	C	F
7	G	F
6	C	F
5	C	F
4	A	F
3	A	B
2	A	B
1		B

14 13 12 11 10 9 8 7 6 5 4 3 2 1   CC MC

CHART D

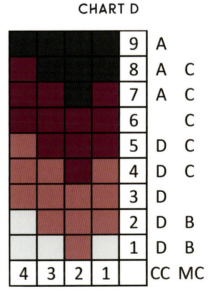

				9	A	
				8	A	C
				7	A	C
				6		C
				5	D	C
				4	D	C
				3	D	
				2	D	B
				1	D	B
4	3	2	1		CC	MC

KEY:
● = *Purl*

Crown

Begin working from Round 1 of Chart E, working the 16-stitch repeat 6 (7, 8) times in total around. Continue working from Chart E as set, changing colors where indicated, until all 17 rounds are complete. 12 (14, 16) sts.

Next Round: Using A (MC), *K2tog; repeat from * to end of round. 6 (7, 8) sts.

Break both yarns, leaving tails, and thread them onto a tapestry needle. Run the tails through the remaining stitches to close the crown. Tie securely.

Finishing

Weave in all the ends. Hand wash and rinse in warm water. Wrap in a towel to remove excess water or use a very light spin in a washing machine. Stretch over a pudding bowl of a suitable size and leave until dry. If ribbing becomes too stretched, this can be pulled in again using steam if necessary.

CHART E

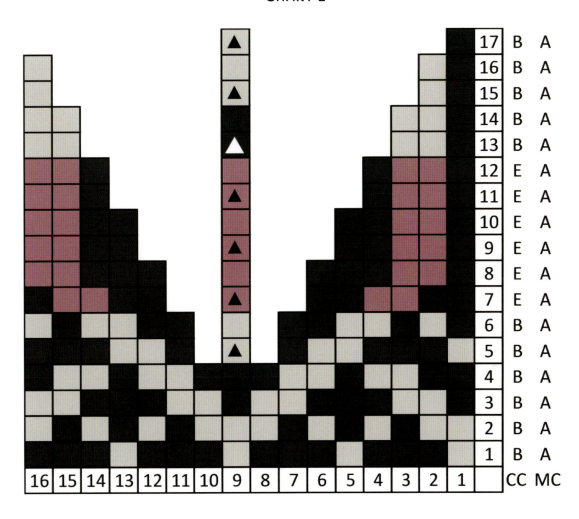

KEY:
Δ = *CDD*

TOOSIK TOORIE

Toosik Toorie was designed to match the Toosik Baby Toorie (page 62), so that parent and child can have a matching set. Coordinating a look between family members not only looks cute, but the hats are also very practical and warm to wear.

×××××
××××××××××××××××××××××××××××

YARN

- Jamieson's of Shetland Spindrift, 100% Shetland wool in 114 yards (105m)/25g balls.
- Yarns A, B, C, D, E, F, and G: 1 ball of each, listed in the color chart.

NEEDLES

- US 2.5 (3mm) double-pointed needles or preferred needles for working circumferences in the round. Adjust size if needed to obtain the correct tension.

NOTIONS

- Stitch markers, tapestry needle.

TENSION

- 32 sts and 36 rounds to 4" x 4" (10 x 10cm), in stranded colorwork, after blocking. Please pay particular attention to the required tension and adjust needle size accordingly.

FINISHED MEASUREMENTS

- Circumference (at brim): 19" (48cm)
- Circumference (at body): 21" (53cm)
- Length (from brim to crown): 8½" (21.5cm)

PATTERN NOTES

- Read all charts from right to left using the colors suggested or colors of your choosing.

××××××××××××××××××××××××××××

COLOR CHART

		Jamieson's of Shetland
Yarn A (MC)		Shade 1340 (Cosmos)
Yarn B		Shade 127 (Pebble)
Yarn C		Shade 293 (Port Wine)
Yarn D		Shade 556 (Old Rose)
Yarn E		Shade 603 (Pot-Pourri)
Yarn F		Shade 104 (Natural White)
Yarn G		Shade 580 (Cherry)

INSTRUCTIONS

Brim

Using A (MC), cast on 152 sts, placing 76 sts on each of two needles to knit in the round. If using circular needles, pm to mark the beginning of the round.

Begin working from Round 1 of Chart A, working the four-stitch repeat 38 times in total around. Continue working from Chart A as set, changing colors where indicated, until all 10 rounds are complete.

Break off B (CC) and continue with A (MC).

Round 11: Knit to end of round.

Inc Round: K4, *K8, KFB; repeat from * to last 4 sts, K4. *168 sts.*

Body

Begin working from Round 1 of Chart B, working the four-stitch repeat 42 times in total around. Continue working from Chart B as set, changing colors where indicated, until all 12 rounds are complete.

Break off E (CC) and continue with B.

Begin working from Round 1 of Chart C, working the 14-stitch repeat 12 times in total around. Continue working from Chart C as set, changing colors where indicated, until all 13 rounds are complete.

Break off A (CC) and continue with B.

Begin working from Round 1 of Chart D, working the four-stitch repeat 42 times in total around. Continue working from Chart D as set, changing colors where indicated, until all 13 rounds are complete.

CHART A

	4	3	2	1		CC	MC
10						B	A
9						B	A
8						B	A
7						E	A
6						E	A
5						E	A
4						B	A
3						B	A
2						B	A
1						B	A

CHART B

	4	3	2	1		CC	MC
12							B
11						E	B
10						E	B
9						E	
8						E	D
7						E	D
6							D
5						C	D
4						C	D
3						C	
2						C	A
1						C	A

CHART C

	14	13	12	11	10	9	8	7	6	5	4	3	2	1		CC	MC
13																	B
12																A	B
11																A	B
10																A	F
9																C	F
8																C	F
7																G	F
6																C	F
5																C	F
4																A	F
3																A	B
2																A	B
1																	B

CHART D

	4	3	2	1		CC	MC
13							A
12						C	A
11						C	A
10						C	
9						C	D
8						C	D
7							D
6						E	D
5						E	D
4						E	
3						E	B
2						E	B
1							B

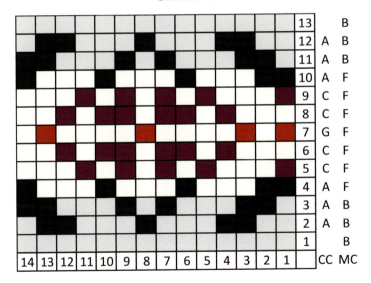

KEY:
• = *Purl*

Crown

Break off C (CC) and continue with A.

Dec Round: *K10, K2tog; repeat from * to end of round. *154 sts.*

Begin working from Round 1 of Chart E, working the 22-stitch repeat seven times in total around. Continue working from Chart E as set, changing colors where indicated, until all 25 rounds are complete. *14 sts.*

Next Round: Using A (MC), *K2tog tbl; repeat from * to end of round. *7 sts.*

Break both yarns, leaving tails, and thread onto tapestry needle. Run the tails through the remaining 7 stitches to close the crown. Tie securely.

Finishing

Weave in all the ends. Hand wash and rinse in warm water. Wrap in a towel to remove excess water or use a very light spin in a washing machine. Stretch over a pudding bowl of a suitable size and leave until dry. If ribbing becomes too stretched, this can be pulled in again using steam if necessary.

CHART E

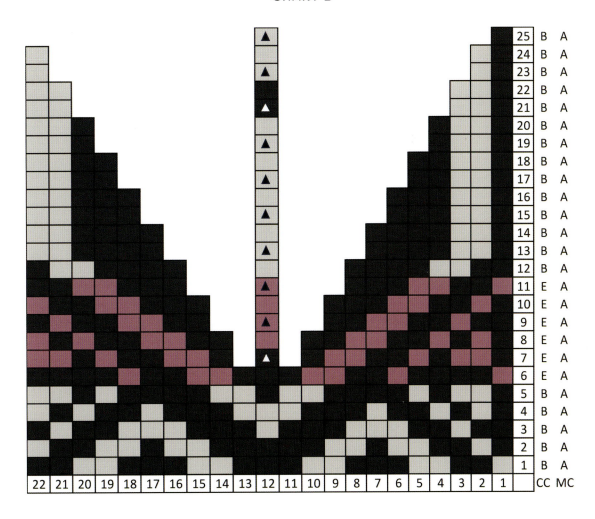

KEY:
Δ = CDD

OORMEL MITTENS

The Oormel Mittens are small and quick to knit, suitable for both beginners and those experienced in Fair Isle knitting. Children of my generation in Shetland often knitted Fair Isle mittens in school as their starting project. The pattern begins with a simple lace cuff, a variation of the traditional Auld Shell lace pattern. The main body of the mitten has three- and nine-row traditional Shetland motifs, which vary depending on the size you choose. Two sizes are given, but with experience, you can adjust the size by adding more or fewer small motif repeats. The pattern can be knitted in either of the two suggested colorways.

Oormel is an affectionate term used in Shetland, sometimes applied to a small child. It can also literally mean "remainders" or "leftovers." As this project uses only small amounts of yarn, it may be that you have enough to work them in your stash that is left over from other projects.

YARN

- Jamieson's of Shetland Spindrift, 100% Shetland wool in 114 yards (105m)/25g balls.
- Yarns A, B, C, D, and E: 1 ball of each, listed on the color charts. Two colorway options are given.

NEEDLES

- US 2.5 (3mm) double-pointed needles or preferred needles for working in the round. Adjust size if needed to obtain the correct tension.
- US 4 (3.5mm) double-pointed needles or preferred needles for working small circumferences in the round. Adjust needles 0.5mm larger than gauge needles for cast on if needed.
- An extra needle will be needed for three-needle cast off if circular needles are used.

TENSION

- 30 sts and 38 rounds to 4" x 4" (10 x 10cm), in stranded colorwork on US 2.5 (3mm) needles, after blocking. Please pay particular attention to the required tension and adjust needle size accordingly.

NOTIONS

- Stitch markers, waste yarn for thumbs, tapestry needle.

FINISHED MEASUREMENTS

Small
- Circumference (at cuff): 4½" (11cm)
- Circumference (at hand): 5½" (14cm)
- Length: 5¾" (14.5cm)

Medium
- Circumference (at cuff): 5½" (14cm)
- Circumference (at hand): 6¾" (17cm)
- Length: 7¼" (18cm)

PATTERN NOTES

- The lace cuff instructions are written, and the Fair Isle work is charted. Read all charts from right to left using the colors suggested or colors of your choosing. Instructions are given for two sizes, represented by parentheses: Small (Medium).

COLOR CHARTS

COLORWAY 1		
	Jamieson's of Shetland	
Yarn A (MC)		Shade 104 (Natural White)
Yarn B		Shade 685 (Delph)
Yarn C		Shade 680 (Lunar)
Yarn D		Shade 425 (Mustard)
Yarn E		Shade 726 (Prussian)

COLORWAY 2		
	Jamieson's of Shetland	
Yarn A (MC)		Shade 104 (Natural White)
Yarn B		Shade 575 (Lipstick)
Yarn C		Shade 570 (Sorbet)
Yarn D		Shade 478 (Amber)
Yarn E		Shade 870 (Cocoa)

INSTRUCTIONS

Lace Cuff

Using A (MC) and US 4 (3.5mm) needles, cast on 28 (40) stitches, placing 14 (20) sts on each of two needles and join to knit in the round. If using circular needles, pm to mark the beginning of the round.

Setup Round: Purl to end of round.

Change to US 2.5 (3mm) needles.

Round 1: *K1, (yo, K1) 2 (3) times, K2tog 2 (3) times, K1, SKP 2 (3) times, (yo, K1) 2 (3) times; repeat from * once more.

Rounds 2–4: Knit to end of round.

Repeat last four rounds 4 (5) more times.

Hand

Inc Round: K2 (0), *K1 (3), KFB; repeat from * to last 2 (0) sts, K2 (0). *40 (50) sts.*

Pm after first 20 (25) sts if using circular needles.

Rounds 2 and 3: Knit to end of round.

Before proceeding with the hand charts, see instructions below regarding thumb construction on Round 7. Work Rounds 1–21 (1–25) of the appropriate Hand Chart. (Thumb shaping is reversed for left hand.)

Thumb Construction (Both Sizes, Both Hands)

The green line on the Hand Chart indicates the 6 (8) sts that will be picked up later to create the thumb. Work as per the Hand Chart up to Round 6, then work as follows:

Round 7: Work to where the thumb sts are marked with a green line, knit the next 6 (8) sts using waste yarn (it should be of a contrasting color to see it when you cut it). Move these sts just worked back onto the left-hand needle, and work over them again in pattern as you continue to follow Round 7 of the Hand Chart. After completion of the charts, break off CC (E or B).

Next 3 rounds: Continuing in A (MC), knit to end of round but stop working before knitting the last st on the last round.

Top Decreases

The top decreases are worked every second round as follows:

Round 1: Slip unworked st from previous round to right-hand needle, K3tog, knit to 1 st before marker or end of Needle 1, pm (if using markers), move last st to Needle 2 if needed, K3tog (removing old marker if markers are used), knit to end of round. *4 sts dec.*

Round 2: Knit to last st, leaving last st unworked.

The last two rounds set the decrease pattern.

Repeat Rounds 1 and 2 a further 3 (5) times, followed by Round 1 once more. *20 (22) sts, 10 (11) sts on each side.*

Turn your work inside out. Join the top of mitten using the three-needle cast-off method.

SMALL RIGHT HAND CHART

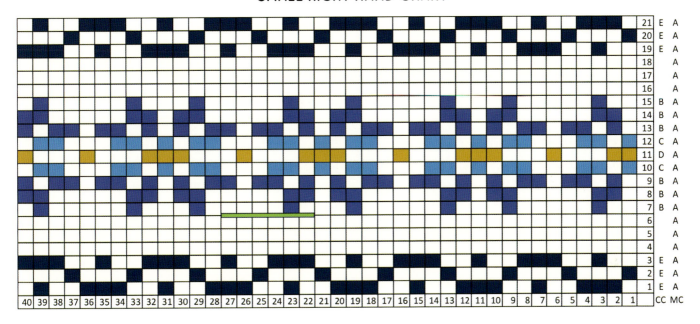

SMALL LEFT HAND CHART

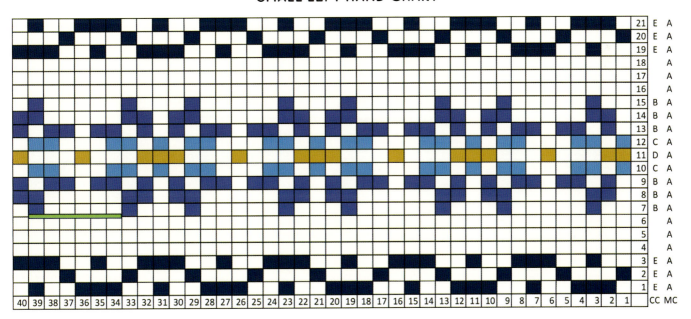

Thumbs (Both Hands)

Setup: Without working sts, starting at lower edge, *pick up the right leg of the stitch just before the waste yarn, then pick up the 6 (8) sts below the waste yarn, followed by one more after the waste yarn.* Turn your work upside down so that the upper side of the thumb is showing. Repeat between * and * once more. Arrange your sts ready to work in the round. Using sharp scissors, carefully snip out the waste yarn. Join in A (MC).

Round 1: Knit to end of round. *16 (20) sts.*

Round 2:

   Small Only: *K6, K2tog; repeat from * once more. *14 sts.*

   Medium Only: *K2tog, K6, K2tog; repeat from * once more. *16 sts.*

Rounds 3–12: Knit to end of round.

Small Only:

   Round 13: *K1, K2tog tbl, K2, K2tog, K1; repeat from * once more. *12 sts.*

   Round 14: *K1, K2tog tbl, K1, K2tog; repeat from * once more. *8 sts.*

   Round 15: *K2tog tbl, K2tog; repeat from * once more. *4 sts.*

   Break yarn and thread through remaining sts to close the thumb. Tie securely and weave in the end.

Medium Only:

   Rounds 13–15: Knit to end of round.

   Round 16: *K2, K2tog tbl, K3, K2tog, K1; repeat from * once more. *16 sts.*

   Round 17: *K1, K2tog tbl, K2, K2tog, K1; repeat from * once more. *12 sts.*

   Round 18: *K1, K2tog tbl, K1, K2tog; repeat from * once more. *8 sts.*

   Break yarn and thread through remaining sts to close the thumb. Tie securely and weave in the end.

Finishing

Weave in the ends. Close any small gaps that develop at the side of the thumb in A (MC).
Hand wash and rinse in warm water. Wrap in a towel to remove excess water or use a very light spin in a washing machine. Ideally, stretch on mitten boards if you have them, or pull to shape and dry flat on clean, dry towels.

MEDIUM RIGHT HAND CHART

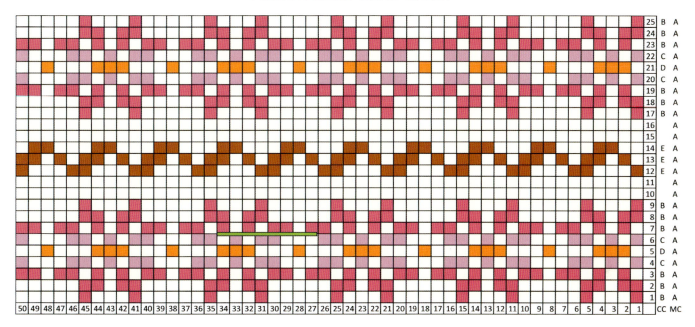

MEDIUM LEFT HAND CHART

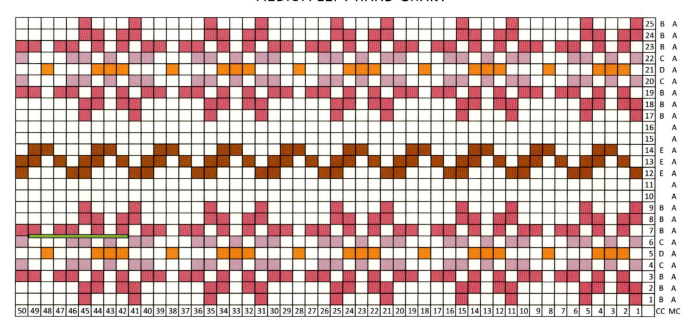

SKALVA SMUCKS

These slippers, or *smucks* as we say in Shetland, are made from Aran-weight Shetland wool, so they knit up quickly and provide thickly padded comfort underfoot. The design features a large snowflake on the top of the foot and heel, perfect for wearing in the depths of winter or over the festive period. The Skalva Smucks are named from the Shetland word *skalva*, which is used to describe snow falling in large flakes.

YARN

- Jamieson's of Shetland Heather Aran, 100% Shetland wool in 100 yards (92m)/50g balls.
- Yarn A: 2 balls; Yarn B: 1 ball, listed in the color chart.

NEEDLES

- US 2.5 (3mm) double-pointed needles or preferred needles for working small circumferences in the round. Adjust needles 0.5mm smaller than gauge needles for ribbing if needed.
- US 4 (3.5mm) double-pointed needles or preferred needles for working small circumferences in the round. Adjust size if needed to obtain the correct tension.
- An extra needle will be needed for three-needle cast off if circular needles are used.

TENSION

- 26 sts and 26 rounds to 4" x 4" (10 x 10cm), in stranded colorwork on US 4 (3.5mm) needles, after blocking. Please pay particular attention to the required tension and adjust needle size accordingly.

FINISHED MEASUREMENTS

US Shoe Size 6–8 (UK 5–7)
- Foot Circumference: 9½" (24cm)
- Length: 10½" (27cm)

US Shoe Size 8–10 (UK 7–9)
- Foot Circumference: 10" (25.5cm)
- Length: 11" (28cm)

NOTIONS

- Stitch markers, tapestry needle.

PATTERN NOTES

- Skalva Smucks are knitted flat from the back of the foot and down under the heel. Stitches are then cast on over the top of the foot, and from there, the foot is worked in the round to the toes. A three-needle cast off is worked at the toe. The sides of the heel are then seamed closed. The ribbing around the foot is worked at the same time as stitches are picked up from the smuck.
- Two sizes are given—Shoe Size 8–10 gives a deeper heel, larger foot circumference, and a slightly longer foot length. Instructions are given for two sizes, represented by parentheses: Shoe Size 6–8 (Size 8–10). There are also instructions for lengthening the smuck to help customize it to your size. If your tension is correct, then adding four rounds will add approximately ½" (1.5cm) to the length. Adding in multiples of four rounds will ensure that the toe chart for the sole will still work with the pattern repeat.
- The heel is worked flat—read charted RS (odd-numbered) rows from right to left, and WS (even-numbered) rows from left to right. Knit the last stitch of each row with both colors to help maintain even tension in the colorwork. In the heel section, the first stitch of each row is slipped purlwise to make it easier to pick up and knit stitches later for the ribbing. Charts C, D, and E are worked in the round—read every round from right to left.

COLOR CHART

		Jamieson's of Shetland
Yarn A (MC)		Shade 323 (Cardinal)
Yarn B		Shade 343 (Ivory)

Heel (worked flat)

Using A (MC) and US 4 (3.5mm) needles, cast on 31 (33) sts.

Row 1 (RS): Knit to end of row.

Row 2 (WS): Purl to end of row.

Working from Chart A, begin at Row 3 for Shoe Size 6–8 (omitting the decreases on the first Row 3 of the Chart) and Row 1 for Shoe Size 8–10. Work the last stitch (the selvage stitch) of every row in both colors to ensure even tension in the colorwork. The first stitch of every row (the stitch worked in both colors) is slipped at the beginning of each row (with yarn held to the WS of the work) to give a neat edge for picking up stitches later.

Continuing working from Chart A, working the indicated decreases until Row 20 is complete. *15 (15) sts.*

Continue working from Chart A, working the indicated increases using M1R and M1L on RS rows, until Row 36 (38) is complete. *31 (33) sts.*

Begin working from Chart B (for your size), continuing to knit the last st of the row with both yarns, and slip the first st of the row with the yarn held to the WS of the work. Repeat Rows 1–4 of Chart B a total of three times, or for a total of 12 rows.

CHART B (SIZE 6-8)

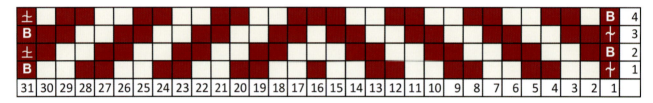

CHART B (SIZE 8-10)

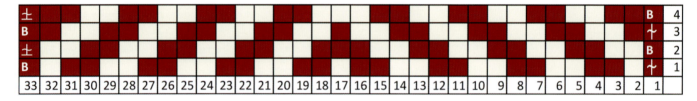

Foot (worked in the round)

Next Round: Work Round 1 of Chart C (for your size) over the 31 (33) sts. At the end of the row, do not turn but break B and using A (MC), cast on 31 (33) sts. Join to work in the round. *62 (66) sts.*

Next Round: Work Round 2 of Chart C (for your size) over first 31 (33) sts, breaking B at the end of Chart C. Work the 31 (33) sts for upper foot in A (MC) only.

Note: If you need a longer foot, this is where you can add some more rounds, just continue to break B at the end of the sole sts and work the upper foot in A (MC) only. If your tension is correct, adding four rounds (one repeat of Chart C—working Rounds 3 and 4, then Rounds 1 and 2—to keep the pattern correct) will add approximately ½" (1.5cm) to the length. If you add length, end with a Round 2 of Chart C.

Be aware that adding more rounds here will also make the foot opening larger—if it ends up too wide, you can adapt the opening later when you pick up for the ribbing. At this point, it may be worth stopping to try on your smucks to see how the foot opening works for you.

CHART A

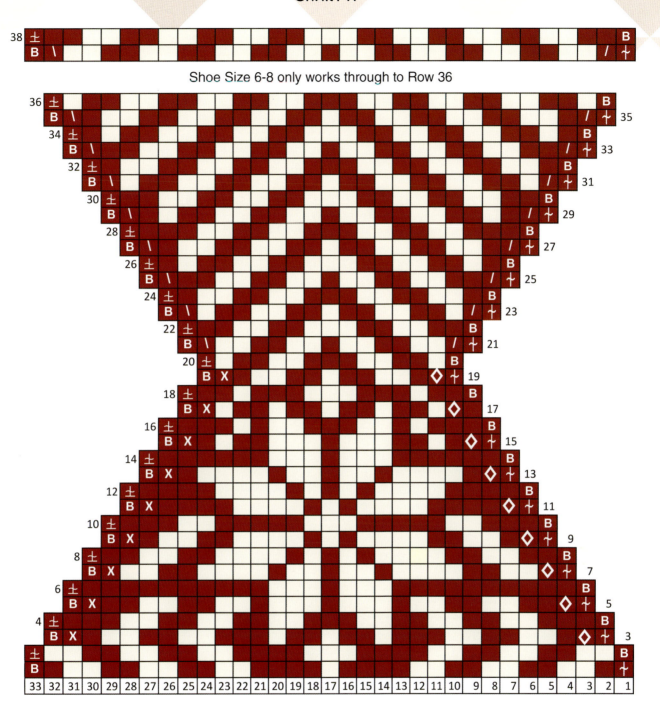

Shoe Size 6-8 only works through to Row 36

KEY:

B = *Work stitch in both colors*

X = *K2tog*

**** = *M1L*

/ = *M1R*

† = *Slip purlwise with yarn at back*

± = *Slip purlwise with yarn at front*

◊ = *SKP*

Λ = *SK2P*

CHART C (SIZE 6-8)

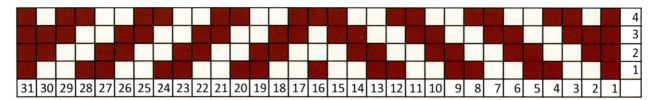

| 31 | 30 | 29 | 28 | 27 | 26 | 25 | 24 | 23 | 22 | 21 | 20 | 19 | 18 | 17 | 16 | 15 | 14 | 13 | 12 | 11 | 10 | 9 | 8 | 7 | 6 | 5 | 4 | 3 | 2 | 1 | | |

CHART C (SIZE 8-10)

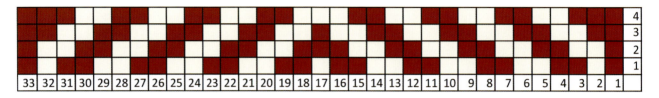

| 33 | 32 | 31 | 30 | 29 | 28 | 27 | 26 | 25 | 24 | 23 | 22 | 21 | 20 | 19 | 18 | 17 | 16 | 15 | 14 | 13 | 12 | 11 | 10 | 9 | 8 | 7 | 6 | 5 | 4 | 3 | 2 | 1 | |

Foot (resumed)

Begin working from Round 3 of Chart C for sole sts and from Round 1 of Chart D for upper foot sts, reading every round from right to left and working Chart C for your size, and the stitches for your size on Chart D (sts 2–32 for Size 6–8; sts 1–33 for Size 8–10). Continue working from Charts C and D as set until Round 26 of Chart D is complete.

CHART D

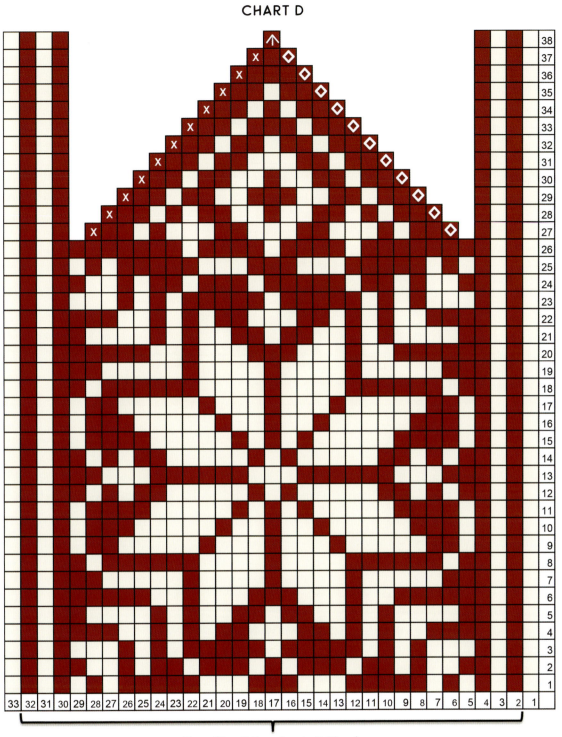

Shoe Size 6-8 works sts 2-32 only

KEY:

X = K2tog

◊ = SKP

⋀ = SK2P

Toe

Begin working from Round 27 of Chart E for sole sts (the toe charts are numbered to match with the rounds of Chart D), working the stitches for your size, and continuing to work from Chart D for upper foot sts as set. Work Charts E and D as set, working the decreases where indicated, until Round 38 is complete. *14 (18) sts.* Turn your work to the WS and with A (MC). Work a three-needle cast off for the remaining 14 (18) sts with 7 (9) sts on each needle.

KEY:

X = K2tog

◊ = SKP

CHART E (SIZE 6-8)

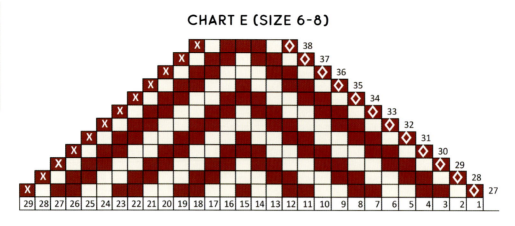

CHART E (SIZE 8-10)

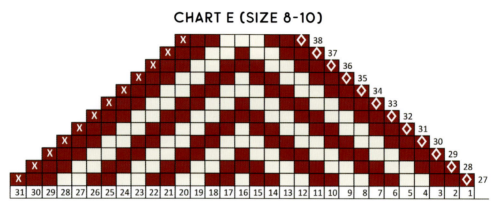

Seaming

Weave in any ends and use mattress stitch to seam up the sides of the heel to hide the selvage stitches.

Ribbing

Using US 2.5 (3mm) and A (MC), cast on 5 sts.

Note: You will knit on the ribbing as you pick up stitches and knit them together with the ribbing. Begin with the cast-on edge of the heel, in the middle.

Row 1 (RS): Sl1wyib, P1, K1, P1, K1, pick up and knit 1 st from work. *6 sts.*

Row 2 (WS): P2tog, K1, P1, K2. *5 sts.*

Continue working Rows 1 and 2 as you work around the smuck opening, picking up one st for every 2 sts along the cast-on edges of the back of the heel and the upper foot, and picking up one st for every slipped st along the side of the sole.

At this point, if you need to draw in the foot opening a little (if it's slightly too big for you), you can pick up 2 sts at once at the corners at the end of a Row 1, and then P3tog at the beginning of the following Row 2. When you have worked around to the back of the foot, ending with a Row 2, cast off all stitches, then sew the cast-on edge to the cast-off edge.

Finishing

Weave in any remaining ends. Hand wash and rinse in warm water. Wrap in a towel to remove excess water or use a very light spin in a washing machine. Stretch smucks on wooden boards or stiff cardboard cut to size and covered with plastic wrap.

HENTILAGETS HAT

Purebred Shetland sheep naturally shed their fleece in spring. The growth of new fleece causes a weak point where the fleece easily separates. During summertime in Shetland, you will find these tufts of wool caught in the heather or against fenceposts where the sheep have rubbed. These fallen bits of wool are known in Shetland as hentilagets, coming from the Norse words *hentan* (pick up) and *laget* (tuft of wool).

Whenever I'm out for a walk, I can't resist picking up hentilagets that lie strewn about. The most striking, naturally coloured hentilagets I have gathered come from the island of Foula, which is famous for its exceptionally pure strain of native Shetland sheep. The sheep there are completely unmodernized and therefore characterized by their diversity of colors and distinct markings.

YARN

- Jamieson's of Shetland Spindrift, 100% Shetland wool in 114 yards (105m)/25g balls.
- Yarns A, B, C, D, E, F, G, H, and I: 1 ball of each, listed in the color chart.

NEEDLES

- US 2.5 (3mm) double-pointed needles or preferred needles for working in the round. Adjust size if needed to obtain the correct tension.

NOTIONS

- Stitch markers, tapestry needle.

TENSION

- 33 sts and 38 rounds to 4" x 4" (10 x 10cm), in stranded colorwork, after blocking. Please pay particular attention to the required tension and adjust needle size accordingly.

FINISHED MEASUREMENTS

- Circumference (at brim): 18½" (47cm)
- Circumference (at body): 20½" (52cm)
- Length (from brim to crown): 8" (20cm)

PATTERN NOTES

- Work all charts from right to left using the colors suggested or colors of your choosing.

COLOR CHART

		Jamieson's of Shetland
Yarn A (MC)		Shade 320 (Steel)
Yarn B		Shade 127 (Pebble)
Yarn C		Shade 104 (Natural White)
Yarn D		Shade 187 (Sunrise)
Yarn E		Shade 587 (Madder)
Yarn F		Shade 578 (Rust)
Yarn G		Shade 1290 (Loganberry)
Yarn H		Shade 308 (Tangerine)
Yarn I		Shade 870 (Cocoa)

INSTRUCTIONS

Using A (MC), cast on 152 sts, placing 76 sts on each of two needles to knit in the round, being careful not to twist your work.

Brim

Begin working from Round 1 of Chart A, working the four-stitch repeat 38 times in total around. Continue working from Chart A as set, changing colors where indicated, until all 10 rounds are complete.
Break off D and continue in A (MC).
Round 11: Continuing in A (MC), knit to end of round.
Inc Round 1: K4, *K8, KFB; repeat from * to last 4 sts, K4. *168 sts*.

Body

Begin working from Round 1 of Chart B, working the six-stitch repeat 28 times in total around. Continue working from Chart B as set, changing colors where indicated, until all nine rounds are complete.
Inc Round 2: Using A (MC), K1, [KFB, K82] twice. *170 sts*.
Begin working from Round 1 of Chart C, working the 34-stitch repeat five times in total around. Continue working from Chart C as set, changing colors where indicated, until all 17 rounds are complete. Break off D.

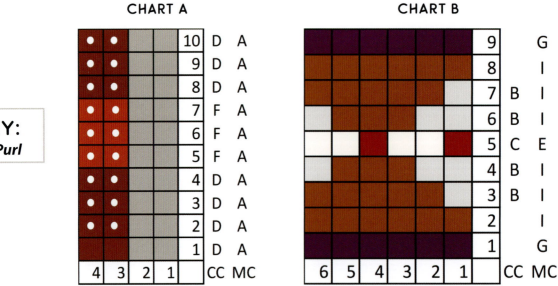

Dec Round 1: Using A (MC), K1, [K2tog, K82] twice. *168 sts.*

Begin working from Round 1 of Chart B, working the six-stitch repeat 28 times in total around. Continue working from Chart B as set, changing colors where indicated, until all nine rounds are complete.

Next Round: Using A (MC), knit to end of round.

Crown

Dec Round 2: Using A (MC), *K4, K2tog; repeat from * to end of round. *140 sts.*

Begin working from Round 1 of Chart D, working the 20-stitch repeat seven times in total around. Continue working from Chart D as set, changing colors where indicated, until all 23 rounds are complete. *14 sts.*

Next Round: Slip the first st of the round to the end of the previous round without knitting it, so that you are starting with a stitch in CC. Using E, [K2tog tbl] to end of round. *7 sts remain.*

Break both yarns, place on tapestry needle, and thread through remaining 7 sts to close crown. Tie securely.

CHART C

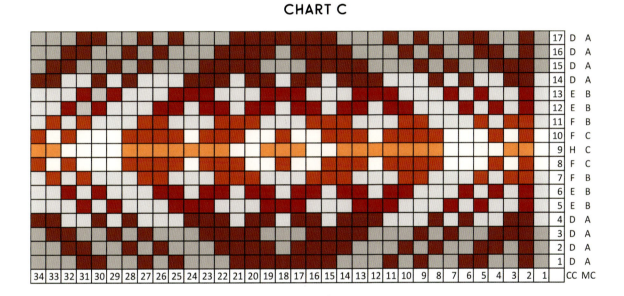

Finishing

Weave in the ends. Hand wash in mild, soapy water and rinse. Wrap in a towel to remove excess water or use a very light spin in a washing machine. Stretch over a pudding bowl of a suitable size and leave until dry. If ribbing becomes too stretched, this can be pulled in again using steam if necessary.

CHART D

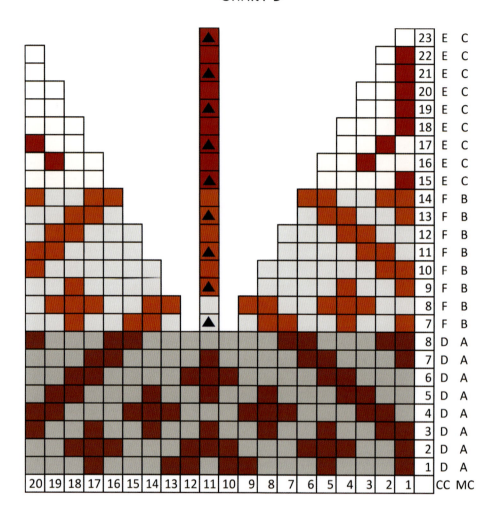

SUKKABURDIE BONNET

Frilly children's bonnets have been popular in Shetland for a long time. My nan made them for me and my sisters in the 1970s, and they are still made for children today. As well as being attractive to look at, they are snug and warm, and they stay in place in the Shetland wind! The bonnet design is offered in two sizes and colorways.

In the past, terms of endearment were not traditionally used, as Shetland people are generally modest and unassuming; however, the word *sukkaburdie* might have been said to a younger child. For instance, a grandmother might address her grandchild as "my peerie sukkaburdie." The literal meaning of this is "my little sugar child."

XXXXXXXXXXXXXXXXXXXXXXXXXXXXXXXXXXXXXXXXXXXXXXXXXXXXXXXXXXXXXXXX

YARN

- Uradale Jumper Weight Organic Unbleached Dyed Yarn, 100% Organic Shetland wool in 94 yards (86m)/25g balls.
- Yarn A: 2 balls; Yarns B, C, D, and E: 1 ball each, listed in the color chart. Two colorway options are given.

NEEDLES

- US 2.5 (3mm) double-pointed needles or preferred needles for working small circumferences in the round. Adjust size if needed to obtain the correct tension.

TENSION

- 32 sts and 38 rounds to 4" x 4" (10 x 10cm), in stranded colorwork, after blocking. Please pay particular attention to the required tension and adjust needle size accordingly.

FINISHED MEASUREMENTS

Size 1 (Age 6 months–2 years)
- Brim circumference: 13¾" (35cm)
- Length from brim to crown 7¾" (20cm)

Size 2 (Age 2–4 years)
- Brim circumference: 15¾" (40cm)
- Length from brim to crown 8¾" (22cm)

NOTIONS

- Stitch markers, tapestry needle.

PATTERN NOTES

- The pattern starts with the frill worked in garter stitch. Then the brim chart begins, which is worked flat. At the end of each row, both yarns are broken and then rejoined to start another right-side row. Tie the two yarn strands together at the beginning and end of each row to secure, but there is no need to weave in the ends. A section of concealed ribbing follows next. The brim will be folded over the ribbing to create a snug fit around the face. Your work is then turned around so that the wrong side becomes the right side. The main body is worked in the round with the addition of a steek. The crown is then worked using center double decreases. Finally, the brim is positioned, and the neckband and straps are added. Steek stitches are not included in stitch counts.
- Read all charts from right to left using the colors suggested or colors of your choosing. The repeated sections are marked within a red box. The charts are displayed in Colorway 1.
- Instructions are given for two sizes, represented by parentheses: Size 1 (Size 2).

XXXXXXXXXXXXXXXXXXXXXXXXXXXXXXXXXXXXXXXXXXXXXXXXXXXXXXXXXXXXXXXX

COLOR CHARTS

COLORWAY 1		
	Uradale Yarns	
Yarn A (MC)		Graeff (Shetland Black)
Yarn B		Bluebell Heath
Yarn C		Speedwell Heath
Yarn D		Angelica
Yarn E		Flukkra (Natural White)

COLORWAY 2		
	Uradale Yarns	
Yarn A (MC)		Forget Me Not Heath
Yarn B		Glansin (Light Grey)
Yarn C		Flukkra (Natural White)
Yarn D		Juniper Heath
Yarn E		Sea Pink Meal

Frill

Using A (MC), cast on 249 (277) sts.
Rows 1–5: Knit to end of row (garter stitch).
Dec Row (RS): Size 1: K4 *K2 tog, K3 tog; repeat from * to last 5 (3) sts, K5 (3). *105 (115) sts.*
Next Row (WS): Knit to end of row.

Brim

Begin working from Row 1 of Chart A. Work the right-hand side sts, then repeat the marked section in the red box a total of 9 (10) times, finishing with the left-hand side sts. For this chart, work with two needles flat. At the end of each row, break the yarns and go back to the start to work another right-side row (brak an eke). Continue working from Chart A as set, changing colors where indicated, until all 15 rows are complete. At the end of Row 15, break yarns ready to start Row 16 on the RS.
Rejoin A (MC).
Row 16 (RS): Knit to the end of the row (it is no longer necessary to break the yarns).
Row 17 (WS): Purl.
Rows 18–19: Repeat Rows 16 and 17 once more.
Dec Row (RS): K5 (1), *K2tog, K6; repeat from * to last 4 (2) sts, K4 (2). *93 (101) sts.*

Concealed Ribbing

Row 1 (WS): Sl1wyif, P1, *K1, P1; repeat from * to last st, K1.
Row 2 (RS): Sl1wyib, *K1, P1; repeat from * to last 2 sts, K2.
Rows 3–14: Repeat Rows 1 and 2 six more times.

This is the bonnet at the ridging stage just before the crown. You can see the brak an eke technique used in the brim, followed by a section of ribbing that will be concealed when the brim is folded over. The main body of the bonnet is turned so that the wrong side is now the right side. Steek stitches can be identified at the right-hand side of the body.

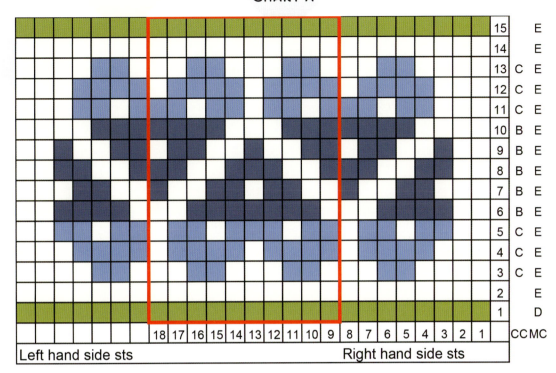

15	E
14	E
13	C E
12	C E
11	C E
10	B E
9	B E
8	B E
7	B E
6	B E
5	C E
4	C E
3	C E
2	E
1	D

18 17 16 15 14 13 12 11 10 | 9 | 8 7 6 5 4 3 2 1 | CC MC

Left hand side sts   Right hand side sts

Body

Turn your work so that from here the wrong side is now the right side. When your hat is complete, the brim will be folded back so the right side is out again (as shown on the opposite page).

Row 1 (new RS): Sl1wyib, knit to end of row.

Row 2 (new WS): Sl1wyif, purl to end of row.

Inc Row (RS): Sl1wyib, K6 (2), *KFB, K3; repeat from * to last 6 (2) sts, K6 (2). *113 (125) sts.*

Next Row: Sl1wyif, purl to end of row.

Note: Please read the entire section below before starting. The instructions explain how to add a steek and join to work in the round.

Arrange your sts ready to work in the round. If working on DPNs, add 56 (63) sts to Needle 1 and 57 (62) sts to Needle 2. Follow the correct Chart B for the size you are making.

Begin working from Round 1 of Chart B. Work sts 1–22, then work the repeated section within the red box a further four (five) times, finishing with left-hand side sts. Pm, then cast on 8 steek sts as [K1A, K1C] twice, [K1C, K1A] twice, as shown on Chart C, pm and join to work in the round. *121 (133) sts.*

Continue working from Chart B as set, changing colors where indicated and working Chart C over steek sts, until all 10 rounds are complete. Repeat Rounds 1–10 two (three) times more, or for 30 (40) total rounds.

If working with DPNs, the 8 steek sts can be divided with 4 on each needle once they have been knitted over.

Next Round: Break off D (CC). Using A (MC), knit to end of round.

In the next round, you will cast off steek sts and set the number of sts for the crown.

Next Round:

   Size 1 Only: Cast off 4 steek sts, rm, K2, *K2tog, K20; repeat from * to last st before marker, K1, rm, cast off 4 steek sts. *108 sts.*

   Size 2 Only: Cast off 4 steek sts, rm, K3, KFB, knit to marker, rm, cast off 4 steek sts. *126 sts.*

CHART B (SIZE 1)

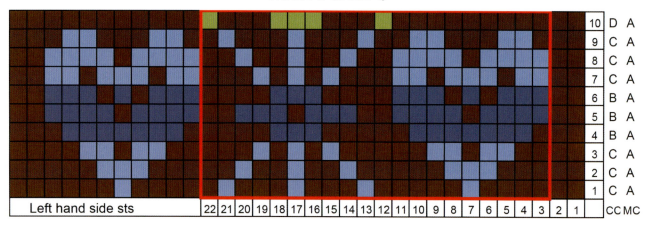

10	D	A
9	C	A
8	C	A
7	C	A
6	B	A
5	B	A
4	B	A
3	C	A
2	C	A
1	C	A

Left hand side sts | 22 21 20 19 18 17 16 15 14 13 12 11 10 9 8 7 6 5 4 3 2 1 | CC MC

CHART B (SIZE 2)

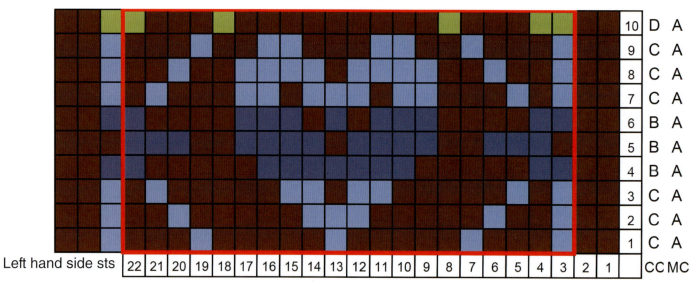

10	D	A
9	C	A
8	C	A
7	C	A
6	B	A
5	B	A
4	B	A
3	C	A
2	C	A
1	C	A

Left hand side sts | 22 21 20 19 18 17 16 15 14 13 12 11 10 9 8 7 6 5 4 3 2 1 | CC MC

Ridging

Continue to work in the round, now without a steek.
Using yarn E:
Round 1: Knit to end of round.
Round 2: Purl to end of round.

Crown

Next Round: Using A (MC), knit to end of round.
Begin working from Round 1 of Chart D, working the 18-stitch repeat six (seven) times in the round.
Continue working from Chart D as set, changing colors where indicated, until all 20 rounds are complete. *12 (14) sts.*
Next Round: Using A (MC), *K2tog; repeat from * to end of round. *6 (7) sts remain.*
Break both yarns, leaving a tail, and thread through remaining 6 (7) stitches to close crown. Tie securely.

CHART C

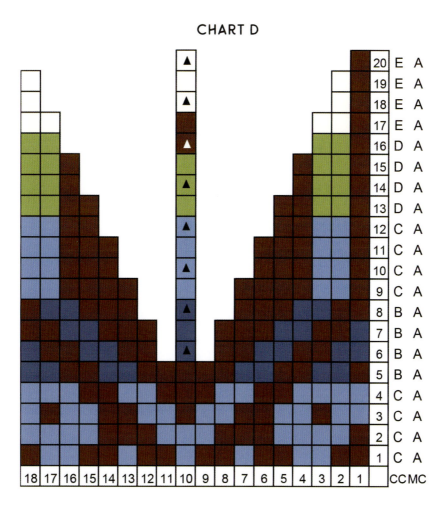

CHART D

KEY:
Δ = CDD

Cut the Steeks

Locate the 8 steek sts. Using sharp scissors, cut open the steek between the central stitches to open up the neck. All the knots and ends of yarn from center of steek can now be removed. Roll the edges under at either side of the hat, and hand sew the edges in place, making sure you put a sewing stitch into every knitted stitch to secure. If you are using Shetland wool, there is no need to reinforce edges before cutting.

Position the Brim

Make sure that all the knots are tight at the edges of the brim, and trim to ¾"–1¼" (2–3cm). Fold the brim over the ribbing so that the frill is positioned between the brim pattern and the main body pattern. The fold should be around the middle of the stocking stitch section after Chart A. The trimmed ends will be tucked in between the two layers of fabric, so there is no need to weave them in. Stitch the brim lengthwise in place.

Neckband

With RS facing, and using A (MC), starting at the front-left side (as worn) of the brim, pick up and knit 9 sts through both layers of fabric at the brim, then pick up a further 51 (59) sts along the lower edge of the hat, followed by another 9 sts through both layers of fabric at the other end. *69 (77) sts.*

Row 1 (WS): Sl1wyif, P1, *K1, P1; repeat from * to last st, K1.
Row 2 (RS): Sl1wyib * K1, P1; repeat from * to last 2 sts, K2.
Repeat Rows 1 and 2 four more times.
Cast off loosely in a rib pattern.

NOTE
It is fine to be a little flexible about the number of sts picked up. Sometimes it is necessary to pick up more than the stated number to ensure there are no gaps in your work. If this happens, reduce to the correct number on the next row of work.

Straps

With RS of right side (as worn) of the hat facing and using A (MC), pick up and knit 6 sts from the edge of the neckband (along the side of the ribbing) and 1 st from the edge of the brim. *7 sts.*

The straps are knitted in garter stitch, knitting every row.

Rows 1–64 (82): Sl1wyib, knit to end of row.

Dec Row 1: Sl1wyib, K2tog, K1, K2tog, K1. *5 sts.*

Dec Row 2: Sl1wyib, K2tog twice. *3 sts.*

Dec Row 3: Sl1wyib, K2tog. *2 sts.*

Dec Row 4: K2tog. *1 st.*

Break yarn and draw through remaining st.

Repeat on other side, picking up 1 st from the brim edge and 6 sts from the edge of the neckband.

Finishing

Weave in any ends in the crown, neckband, and straps. Stitch any small holes that appear where the ridging joins the neck band at the back.

Hand wash and rinse in warm water. Wrap in a towel to remove excess water or use a very light spin in a washing machine. Stretch over a ball or balloon of a suitable size, and leave until dry. If ribbing becomes too stretched, this can be pulled in again using steam if necessary.

LYRA HAT

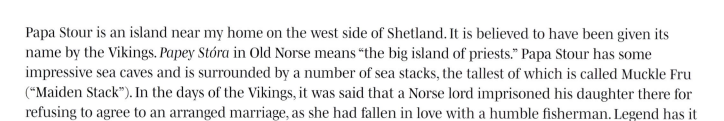

Papa Stour is an island near my home on the west side of Shetland. It is believed to have been given its name by the Vikings. *Papey Stóra* in Old Norse means "the big island of priests." Papa Stour has some impressive sea caves and is surrounded by a number of sea stacks, the tallest of which is called Muckle Fru ("Maiden Stack"). In the days of the Vikings, it was said that a Norse lord imprisoned his daughter there for refusing to agree to an arranged marriage, as she had fallen in love with a humble fisherman. Legend has it that her lover rescued her from solitary confinement on top of the sea stack, and they fled away together.

Another two imposing sea stacks are called Lyra Skerry and Fugla Skerry. Lyra (pronounced *leera*) comes from the word *leerie*, the Shetland word for the Manx shearwater, a seabird. *Fugl* is the Norse word for bird. Sadly, Manx shearwaters are scarce visitors in Shetland now, but these small uninhabited islands remain important undisturbed habitats for many other seabirds.

YARN

- Jamieson & Smith 2ply Jumper Weight, 100% Shetland wool in 114 yards (105m)/25g balls; or Jamieson's of Shetland Spindrift, 100% Shetland wool in 114 yards (105m)/25g balls.
- Yarns A, B, C, D, E, F, G, H, J, and K: 1 ball of each, listed in the color chart.

NEEDLES

- US 2.5 (3mm) double-pointed needles or preferred needles for working in the round. Adjust size if needed to obtain the correct tension.

NOTIONS

- Stitch markers, tapestry needle.

TENSION

- 33 sts and 36 rounds to 4" x 4" (10 x 10cm), in stranded colorwork, after blocking. Please pay particular attention to the required tension and adjust needle size accordingly.

FINISHED MEASUREMENTS

- Brim circumference: 18½" (47cm)
- Body circumference: 20½" (52cm)
- Length from brim to crown: 8¼" (21cm)

PATTERN NOTES

- Read all charts from right to left using the colors suggested or colors of your choosing. The colors used are listed in the columns on the right-hand side of the charts. The background color is listed in the right column and the foreground color in the left column.

COLOR CHART

		Jamieson & Smith	Jamieson's of Shetland
Yarn A (MC)		Shetland Heritage Natural Moorit	Shade 108 (Moorit)
Yarn B		Shade 135 (Mid Navy)	Shade 684 (Cobalt)
Yarn C		Shade FC41 (Dark Teal Blue)	Shade 750 (Petrol)
Yarn D		Shade 5 (Dyed Shetland Black)	Shade 970 (Espresso)
Yarn E		Shade 16 (Bright Bonnie Blue)	Shade 665 (Bluebell)
Yarn F		Shade 1403 (Red)	Shade 595 (Maroon)
Yarn G		Shade 66 (Medium Yellow)	Shade 182 (Buttercup)
Yarn H		Shade 96 (Pale Lemon)	Shade 179 (Buttermilk)
Yarn J		Shade 1A (Natural White)	Shade 104 (Natural White)
Yarn K		Shade 91 (Egg Yolk Yellow)	Shade 1160 (Scotch Broom)

INSTRUCTIONS

Brim

With A (MC), cast on 152 sts, placing 76 sts on each of two needles to knit in the round. If using circular needles, pm to mark the beginning of the round.

Begin working from Round 1 of Chart A, working the four-stitch repeat 38 times in total around. Continue working from Chart A as set, changing colors where indicated, until all 10 rounds are complete. Break off B and continue in A (MC).

Round 11: With A, knit to end of round.

Inc Round: K4, *K8, KFB; repeat from * to last 4 sts, K4. *168 sts.*

Body

Begin working from Round 1 of Chart B, working the 28-stitch repeat six times in total around. Continue working from Chart B as set, changing colors where indicated, until all 35 rounds are complete. The small motif repeats are marked within the green boxes.

At the end of Chart B, break off F and continue to crown with A.

Crown

Round 1: With A, knit to end of round.

Dec Round: *K6, K2tog; repeat from * to end of round. *147 sts.*

Begin working from Round 1 of Chart C, working the 21-stitch repeat seven times in total around. Continue working from Chart C as set, changing colors where indicated, and working decreases beginning on Round 6, until all 23 rounds are complete. *21 sts.*

Next Round: Using A (MC), *K1, K2tog; repeat from * to end of round. *14 sts.*

Next Round: *K2tog; repeat from * to end of round. *7 sts remain.*

Break off A (MC), leaving a tail, and thread through remaining 7 stitches to close the crown. Tie securely.

CHART A

●	●			10	B	A
●	●			9	B	A
●	●			8	B	A
●	●			7	E	A
●	●			6	E	A
●	●			5	E	A
●	●			4	B	A
●	●			3	B	A
●	●			2	B	A
				1	B	A
4	3	2	1		CC	MC

KEY:
● = *Purl*

CHART B

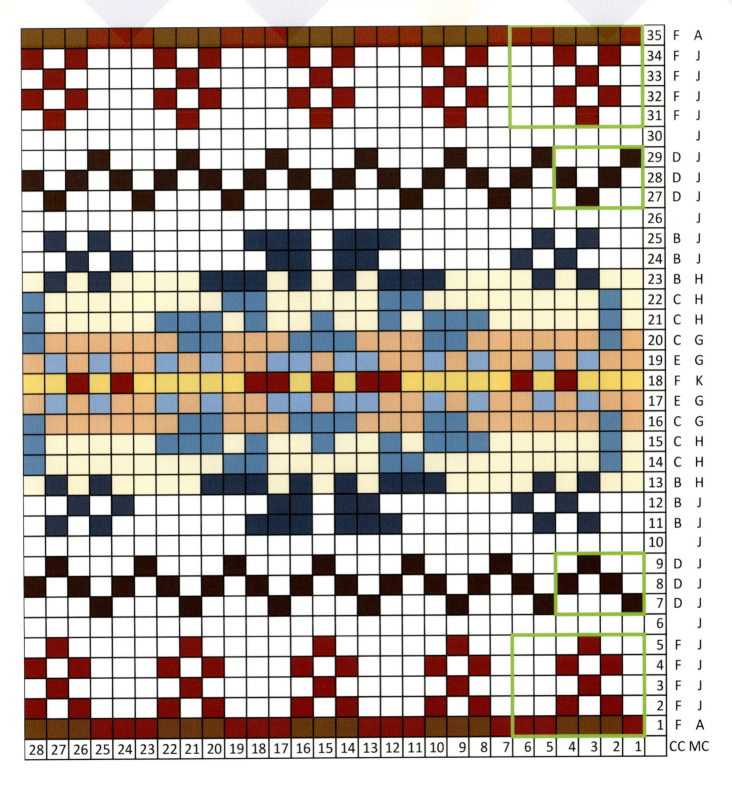

CHART C

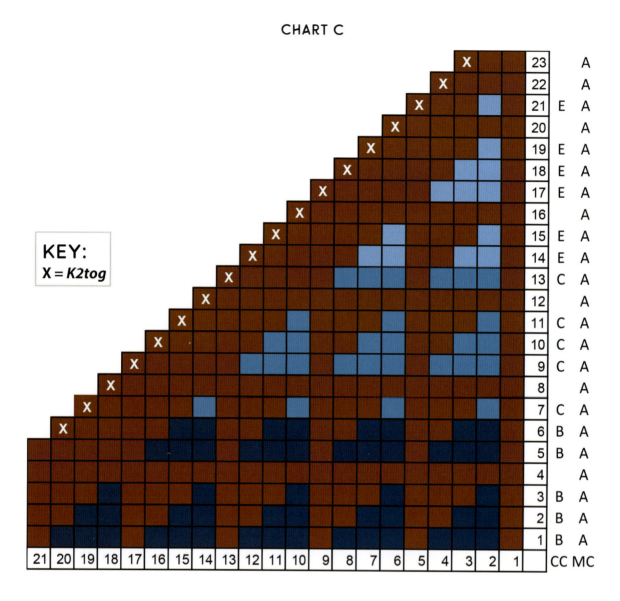

	21	20	19	18	17	16	15	14	13	12	11	10	9	8	7	6	5	4	3	2	1		CC	MC
23																			X			23		A
22																		X				22		A
21																	X					21	E	A
20																X						20		A
19															X							19	E	A
18														X								18	E	A
17													X									17	E	A
16												X										16		A
15											X											15	E	A
14										X												14	E	A
13									X													13	C	A
12								X														12		A
11							X															11	C	A
10						X																10	C	A
9					X																	9	C	A
8				X																		8		A
7			X																			7	C	A
6		X																				6	B	A
5	X																					5	B	A
4																						4		A
3																						3	B	A
2																						2	B	A
1																						1	B	A

KEY:
X = *K2tog*

Finishing

Weave in all the ends. Hand wash and rinse in warm water. Wrap in a towel to remove excess water or use a very light spin in a washing machine. Stretch over a pudding bowl of a suitable size and leave until dry. If ribbing becomes too stretched, this can be pulled in again using steam if necessary.

LYRA MITTS

Cunningsburgh, where my mother's side of the family comes from, is one of the areas in Shetland famed for its highly decorated gloves (see also Klivsi Glivs on page 122). Cunningsburgh gloves most often have turned-up, patterned cuffs, as featured in this design. The folded cuff gives you an attractive design on the outside but with the benefits of ribbing on the inside—the combination of a snug fit around the wrist while maintaining all important pattern and design. Incidentally, this also gives a comfortable and warm double layer around the wrist.

While making the Lyra Mitts, you will also learn how to make another important element in Shetland knitting: the thumb gusset. This is an important feature, as a thumb gusset makes for a more comfortable fit and allows for additional movement when using your thumb.

YARN

- Jamieson & Smith 2ply Jumper Weight, 100% Shetland wool in 114 yards (105m)/25g balls; or Jamieson's of Shetland Spindrift, 100% Shetland wool in 114 yards (105m)/25g balls.
- Yarns A, B, C, D, E, F, G, H, J, and K: 1 ball of each, listed in the color chart.

NEEDLES

- US 2.5 (3mm) double-pointed needles or preferred needles for working small circumferences in the round. Adjust size if needed to obtain the correct tension.

NOTIONS

- Stitch markers, waste yarn for thumbs, tapestry needle.

TENSION

- 36 sts and 38 rounds to 4" x 4" (10 x 10cm), in stranded colorwork, after blocking. Please pay particular attention to the required tension and adjust needle size accordingly.

FINISHED MEASUREMENTS

One Size (Woman's Small Hands)
- Cuff Circumference: 6¼" (16cm)
- Hand Circumference: 6¾" (17cm)
- Length (after cuff is folded): 7¼" (18cm)

PATTERN NOTES

- Read all charts from right to left using the colors suggested or colors of your choosing. The colors used are listed in the columns on the right-hand side of the charts. The background color is listed in the right column and the foreground color in the left column.

COLOR CHART

		Jamieson & Smith	Jamieson's of Shetland
Yarn A (MC)		Shetland Heritage Natural Moorit	Shade 108 (Moorit)
Yarn B		Shade 135 (Mid Navy)	Shade 684 (Cobalt)
Yarn C		Shade FC41 (Dark Teal Blue)	Shade 750 (Petrol)
Yarn D		Shade 5 (Dyed Shetland Black)	Shade 970 (Espresso)
Yarn E		Shade 16 (Bright Bonnie Blue)	Shade 665 (Bluebell)
Yarn F		Shade 1403 (Red)	Shade 595 (Maroon)
Yarn G		Shade 66 (Medium Yellow)	Shade 435 (Apricot)
Yarn H		Shade 96 (Pale Lemon)	Shade 179 (Buttermilk)
Yarn J		Shade 1A (Natural White)	Shade 104 (Natural White)
Yarn K		Shade 91 (Egg Yolk Yellow)	Shade 1160 (Scotch Broom)

INSTRUCTIONS

Cuff

Using A (MC), cast on 52 sts, placing 26 on each of two needles to knit in the round. If using circular needles, pm to mark the beginning of the round.

Rounds 1–4: *K2, P2; repeat from * to end of round.

Inc Round: *K12, KFB; repeat from * to end of round. *56 sts.*

Work Rounds 1–15 of Chart A, working the 28-stitch repeat twice around. The repeated sections of each motif are marked within the green box.

Break off D (CC).

Rounds 16–18: Using A (MC), knit to end of round.

Concealed Ribbing

Turn your work inside out. The wrong side is now the right side of your mitt. You will be knitting back over the last sts knitted. When you have completed your mitt, fold the cuff up so the right side is out again.

Round 1: Using A (MC), knit 1 round. This row creates the ridge where the cuff is folded.

Dec Round: *K12, K2tog; repeat from * to end of round. *52 sts.*

Rounds 3–24: *K2, P2; repeat from * to end of round.

Hand

Inc Round: Using A (MC), pm, K3 *KFB, K2; repeat from * a total of 7 times, K2, pm, K12, KFB, K13. *60 sts, with 33 back of hand sts and 27 palm sts.*

Rounds 2–4: Knit to end of round.

Before proceeding with the Hand Charts, please see instructions below regarding thumb construction over Rounds 11–16 and the decreases in Rounds 26 and 30.

Work Rounds 1–35 of the appropriate Hand Chart. (Thumb shaping is reversed for left hand.) *60 sts.*

Thumb Construction (Both Hands)

The thumb gusset starts with 3 sts and is gradually increased to 9 sts using M1R and M1L as indicated on the Hand Chart. The green line on the charts indicates the 9 sts that will be picked up later to create the thumb. Work as per the chart up to Round 16, then work as follows:

Round 17: Work to where the thumb sts are marked with a green line, knit the next 9 sts using waste yarn (it should be of a contrasting color, so it stands out when you cut it). Move these 9 sts just worked back on to the left-hand needle and work over them again in pattern as you continue to follow Round 17 of the Hand Chart. After thumb increases, you will have 66 sts.

Rounds 26 and 30: Work decreases (K2tog) in these rounds as marked.

Top Edge Ribbing (Both Hands)

Break off CC.

Round 1: Using A (MC), knit to end of round.

Dec Round: K2, *K5, K2tog; repeat from * to last 2 sts, K2. *52 sts.*

Rounds 3–6: *K2, P2; repeat from * to end of round.

Cast off neatly in ribbing.

CHART A

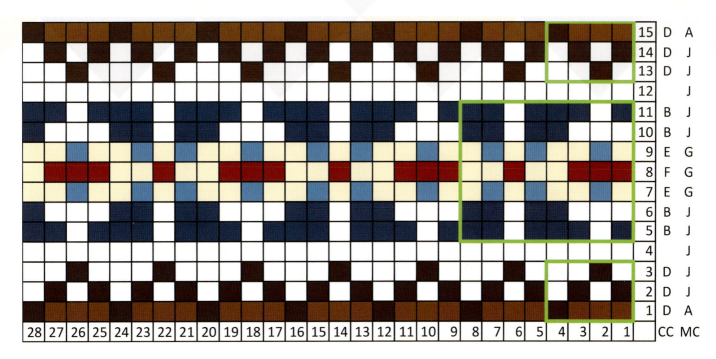

Thumbs (Both Hands)

Setup: Without working sts, starting at the lower edge, *pick up the right leg of the stitch just before the waste yarn, then pick up the 9 sts below the waste yarn, followed by one more after the waste yarn.* Turn your work upside down so that the upper side of the thumb is showing. Repeat between * and * once more. *22 sts.*

Arrange your sts ready to work in the round. Using sharp scissors, carefully snip out the waste yarn. Join in A (MC).

Round 1: *K9, K2tog; repeat from * once more. *20 sts.*

Rounds 2–12: Knit to end of round.

Round 13: K2tog, (P1, K1) four times, P2tog, (K1, P1) four times. *18 sts.*

Rounds 14–16: *K1, P1; repeat from * to end of round.

Cast off neatly in ribbing.

Finishing

Weave in ends. Close any small gaps that develop at the side of the thumb in the appropriate color. Hand wash and rinse in warm water. Wrap in a towel to remove excess water or use a very light spin in a washing machine. Ideally, stretch on glove boards if you have them, or pull to shape and dry flat on clean, dry towels. If top edge ribbing becomes too stretched, this can be pulled in again using steam if necessary.

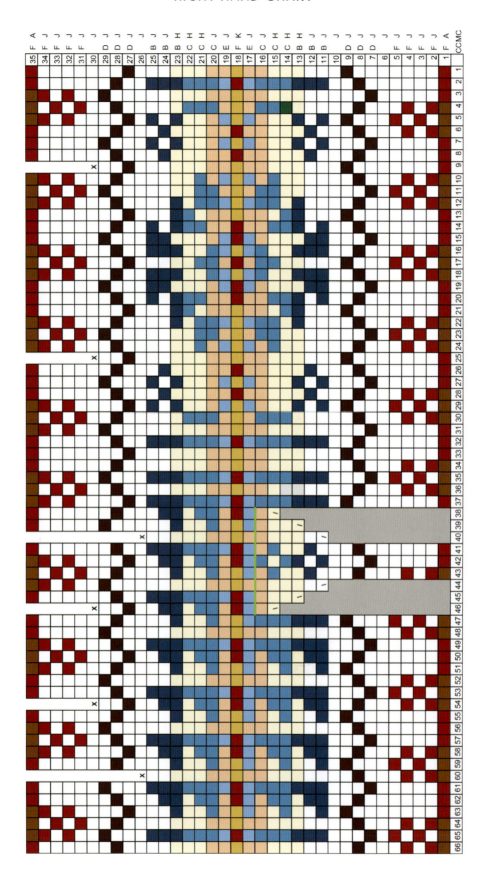

KEY:
/ = M1R

\ = M1L

X = K2tog

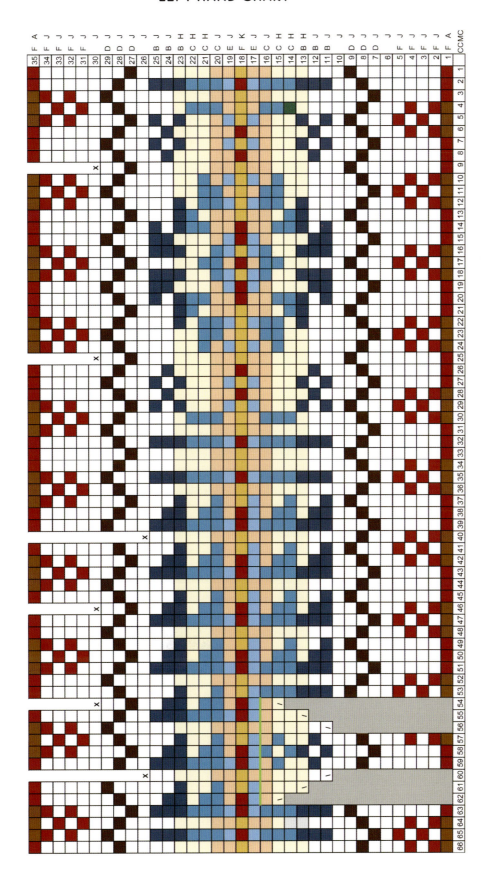

LUND SOCKS

Unst, Shetland's most northerly isle, is thought to be one of the places where the Vikings first landed in the North Atlantic. There are the remains of at least 60 longhouses, the highest density of rural Viking sites anywhere. The area around Lund, in Unst, is a time warp of Norse and Iron Age history. There are the remains of a 56 foot (17m) wide broch (ancient walled structure) with two Viking longhouses nearby, presumably built using the stones from the earlier broch. Finally, there are the remains of Lund Chapel, dating to before the 12th century and built for the Viking settlements nearby. All these sites have been exposed, leaving it to your imagination how life would have been. The Lund Socks were inspired by a camping trip I made to this area.

YARN

- Jamieson's of Shetland Spindrift, 100% Shetland wool in 114 yards (105m)/25g balls.
- Yarns A and D: 2 balls of each; Yarns B, C, E, F, G, H, I, and J: 1 ball of each, listed in the color chart.

NEEDLES

- US 2.5 (3mm) double-pointed needles or preferred needles for working small circumferences in the round. Adjust size if needed to obtain the correct tension.
- An extra needle will be needed for three-needle cast off if circular needles are used.

NOTIONS

- Stitch markers, stitch holder or waste yarn, tapestry needle.

TENSION

- 34 sts and 38 rounds to 4" x 4" (10 x 10cm), in stranded colorwork, after blocking. Please pay particular attention to the required tension and adjust needle size accordingly.

FINISHED MEASUREMENTS

One size (US size 8 [UK size 6])
- Leg Circumference: 9¾" (25cm)
- Foot Circumference: 8¾" (22cm)
- Leg Length (from top to heel flap): 10¾" (27cm)

PATTERN NOTES

- The Lund Socks are one-size socks suitable for wearing around the home. Alternatively, they can be worn as an occasional boot sock, but they are not intended for everyday use, as Shetland wool will not withstand daily wash and wear.
- The socks are worked top down in the round, to the top of the heel. The heel flap is knitted flat and then after the heel is turned, stitches are picked up along the edge of the heel flap and the foot is worked in the round again.
- Instructions are given in the foot section about adding a few rounds to increase the length of the foot. The toe is finished with a three-needle cast off.
- Read all charts from right to left using the colors suggested or colors of your choosing. The colors used are listed in columns on the right-hand side of the charts.

COLOR CHART

		Jamieson's of Shetland
Yarn A (MC)		Shade 320 (Steel)
Yarn B		Shade 122 (Granite)
Yarn C		Shade 127 (Pebble)
Yarn D		Shade 598 (Mulberry)
Yarn E		Shade 293 (Port Wine)

		Jamieson's of Shetland
Yarn F		Shade 596 (Clover)
Yarn G		Shade 610 (Purple)
Yarn H		Shade 179 (Buttermilk)
Yarn I		Shade 104 (Natural White)
Yarn J		Shade 587 (Madder)

INSTRUCTIONS

Cuff

With A (MC), cast on 80 sts and join to knit in the round, being careful not to twist your work. If using circular needles, place a stitch marker to mark the beginning of the round.

Corrugated Ribbing

Work Rounds 1–17 of Chart A from pattern written below or from Chart A.

Round 1: *K2A, K2D; repeat from * to end of round.
Rounds 2–6: *K2A, P2D; repeat from * to end of round.
Rounds 7–11: *K2B, P2E; repeat from * to end of round.
Rounds 12–17: *K2A, P2D; repeat from * to end of round. Break off D (CC).
Round 18: Using A (MC), knit to end of round.
Inc Round: *K19, KFB; repeat from * to end of round. *84 sts.*

Leg

Work Rounds 1–42 of Chart B, repeating the chart twice in the round (front and back are the same). Work Rounds 1–41 once more.

Round 84: Work Round 42 of Chart B, but increase by KFB on stitch number 42 each time you come to it. *86 sts.*

This will take you to the start of the heel. Break off D (CC).

CHART A

•	•			17	D	A
•	•			16	D	A
•	•			15	D	A
•	•			14	D	A
•	•			13	D	A
•	•			12	D	A
•	•			11	E	A
•	•			10	E	A
•	•			9	E	A
•	•			8	E	A
•	•			7	E	A
•	•			6	D	A
•	•			5	D	A
•	•			4	D	A
•	•			3	D	A
•	•			2	D	A
				1	D	A
4	3	2	1		CC	MC

Heel

Divide for heel:

Stitches for upper foot will be referred to as Needle 1, and the stitches for the sole of the foot (heel) will be referred to as Needle 2.

Needle 1: Put Needle 1 (43 sts) on a stitch holder and continue working on Needle 2 (43 sts) only.

Needle 2: With A (MC) and WS facing, purl 43 sts to end of Needle 2 (you will be working back over sts just knitted), turn.

Heel Flap

With RS of Needle 2 sts facing, rejoin D (CC).
Row 1 (RS): Sl1wyib, *K1A, K1D; repeat from * to last 2 sts, K1A, K1tbl A, turn.
Row 2 (WS): Sl1wyif, *P1D, P1A; repeat from * to end of row, turn.
The last two rows set the heel flap pattern, which is also shown on Chart E. Work the last two rows 11 times more, for a total of 24 rows, ending with a WS row. Turn, ready to work a RS row.

Heel Turn

Maintain the colorwork heel pattern while working the short rows/decreases as follows:
Row 1 (RS): Sl1wyib, K26, K3tog tbl, K1, turn. *41 sts on heel.*
Row 2 (WS): Sl1wyif, P12, P3tog, P1, turn. *39 sts.*
Row 3: Sl1wyib, K13, K3tog tbl, K1, turn. *37 sts.*
Row 4: Sl1wyif, P14, P3tog, P1, turn. *35 sts.*
Row 5: Sl1wyib, K15, K3tog tbl, K1, turn. *33 sts.*
Row 6: Sl1wyif, P16, P3tog, P1, turn. *31 sts.*
Row 7: Sl1wyib, K17, K3tog tbl, K1, turn. *29 sts.*
Row 8: Sl1wyif, P18, P3tog, P1, turn. *27 sts.*
Row 9: Sl1wyib, K19, K3tog tbl, K1, turn. *25 sts.*
Row 10: Sl1wyif, P20, P3tog, P1. *23 sts.*
Break off both yarns and secure ends.

Gusset

Please read the entire gusset and foot section before starting.

With RS facing, put 43 Needle 1 sts back on the needles, and join A and D at right side of instep sts. Pm for beginning of round. Chart C is worked on Needle 1 for upper foot. Chart D is worked on Needle 2 for sole. The first 8 sts and last 8 sts of Chart D form the gusset-stripe pattern. These sts are gradually decreased until none remain.

Setup Round:

Needle 1: Work Round 1 of Chart C across instep sts, pm.

Needle 2: Work Round 1 of Chart D as follows: Pick up and knit 8 sts along heel edge as [K1A, K1D], break yarn D, pick up and knit 5 sts using A (these 13 sts are marked in the blue box). Knit across 23 heel sts using A. Pick up and knit 5 sts along the heel edge. Rejoin D, pick up and knit 8 sts to end of round as [K1D, K1A] (these 13 sts are marked in the blue box). *92 sts.*

Round 1 (Dec Round):

Needle 1: Work next round of Chart C to marker, sm.

Needle 2: Work next round of Chart D, repeating the marked section in the red box six times. Use SKP for right-hand-side decreases and K2tog for left-hand-side decreases. *2 sts dec.*

Round 2:

Needle 1: Work next round of Chart C.

Needle 2: Work next round of Chart D, repeating the marked section in red six times.

The last two rounds set the foot and sole pattern and the decrease pattern for the gusset stripe. Continue working from Charts C and D as set, changing background color and decreasing of Chart D as indicated, and working the repeat marked in the red box six times across Needle 2, until Round 22 on both charts is complete, with 43 sts for foot on Needle 1, and 33 sts remaining for the sole on Needle 2. *76 sts.*

CHART B

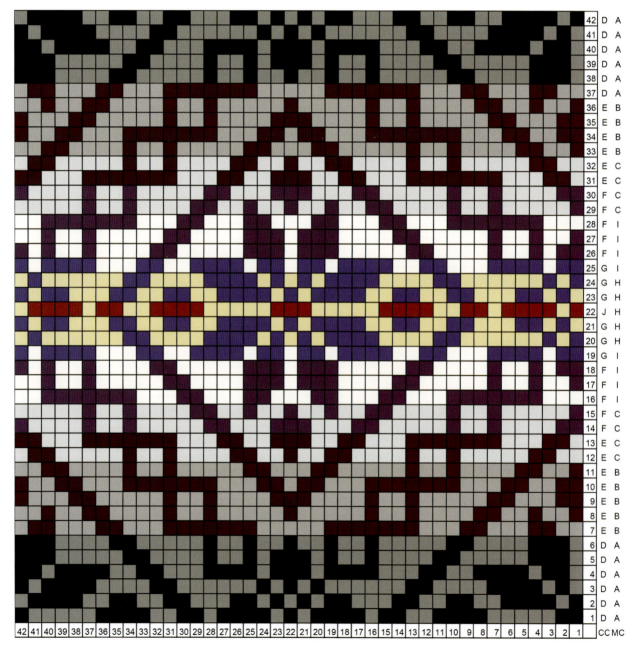

CHART C

Foot

Rounds 20–22 of Chart D set the vertical repeat of the sole sts on Needle 2. Continue working from Charts C and D as set, changing the colors as set by Chart C, until all 56 rounds of Chart C are completed. Please note decreases on Chart C on Round 43 (use SKP for right-hand-side decreases and K2tog for left-hand-side decreases). You will end at the side of the instep, ready to work the sole sts.

At the end of Round 56, 41 sts remain for upper foot on Needle 1 and 33 sts for the sole on Needle 2. *74 sts.* If you wish to add length to the foot, you may do so here. Repeat Rounds 43–56 of Chart C (without the decreases in Round 43) and Rounds 20–22 of Chart D to 1¾" (4.5cm) less than the desired length, ending with a Round 56 of Chart C and ending at the side of the instep ready to work the sole sts.

Toe

Break off D (CC) on Needle 1.

Using A (MC), knit 1 round, rm as you work around. Before proceeding with the toe, please read the entire section regarding toe shaping.

Maintain the colorwork toe pattern (below) while working the decreases in the following rounds.

Setup Round: K1A, *K2tog D, K1A, K1D, K1A; repeat from * to last 3 sts, K3tog D. *58 sts.*

Arrange your stitches so there are 29 sts on each of two needles.

Round 1: Work in toe pattern and stop knitting before working the last st.

Round 2:

Needle 1: Slip the unworked st from previous round onto Needle 1, K3tog, and then continue in toe pattern to the last st of Needle 1.

Needle 2: Slip the unworked st from Needle 1 onto Needle 2, K3tog, and then continue in toe pattern to the end of the round. *4 sts dec.*

Repeat Rounds 1 and 2 a further four times, then continue working Round 2 only on every round four times, or until 22 total sts remain. Turn your work inside out and cast off using the three-needle cast-off method.

Toe Pattern

Round 1: *K1A, K1D; repeat from * to end of round.
Round 2: *K1D, K1A; repeat from * to end of round.

These two rounds set the toe pattern, which is also demonstrated on Chart E.

CHART D

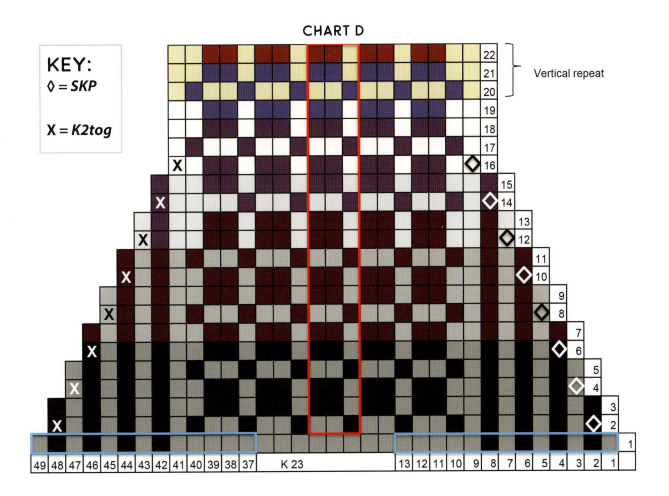

KEY:

◊ = SKP

X = K2tog

Vertical repeat

CHART E

Finishing

Weave in ends. Hand wash and rinse in warm water. Wrap in a towel to remove excess water or use a very light spin in a washing machine. Ideally, stretch on sock boards if available; otherwise, pin to shape or use thick cardboard covered in plastic wrap to shape. Leave to dry. If ribbing becomes too stretched, this can be pulled in again using steam if necessary.

KLIVSI GLIVS

Klivsi Glivs starts with a two-colored patterned cuff; the use of knit and purl stitches gives a textured look. The cuff and the palm pattern are inspired by the distinctive look of designs hailing from the small Scottish town of Sanquhar. The hand features a traditional motif that fits neatly on the back of the hand. *Kliv* is the Norse word for "a cleft in a rock." The same word applies to a hoof or cloven foot; therefore, *klivsi* became the Shetland name for a sheep. *Glivs* is how we would say "gloves" in Shetland!

Cunningsburgh, where my mother's side of the family comes from, is a place in Shetland famed for their gloves. Cunningsburgh gloves are typically complex and highly decorated, having turned-up, patterned cuffs (see Lyra Mitts on page 108) as well as patterned fingers or "double fingers" as they are known, ensuring that every inch is rich in design. Two-colored fingers are tricky to make but well worth the effort in the finished piece.

YARN

- Jamieson & Smith 2ply Jumper Weight, 100% Shetland wool in 114 yards (105m)/25g balls; or Jamieson's of Shetland Spindrift, 100% Shetland wool in 114 yards (105m)/25g balls.
- Yarns A, B, C, D, E, F, G, and H: 1 ball of each, listed in the color chart.

NEEDLES

- US 2.5 (3mm) double-pointed needles or preferred needles for working small circumferences in the round. Adjust size if needed to obtain the correct tension.

NOTIONS

- Waste yarn for thumbs, stitch holders or waste yarn for fingers, tapestry needle.

TENSION

- 34 sts and 33 rounds to 4" x 4" (10 x 10cm), in stranded colorwork, after blocking. Please pay particular attention to the required tension and adjust needle size accordingly.

FINISHED MEASUREMENTS

One Size (Average Woman's Hands)

- Cuff Circumference: 6½" (16.5cm)
- Hand Circumference: 8" (20cm)
- Length (after cuff is folded): 9½" (24cm)

PATTERN NOTES

- The charts are displayed in color with the addition of columns showing the pattern colors to the right of the chart. The background color is listed in the right column and the foreground color in the left column. Read all charts from right to left using the colors suggested or colors of your choosing.
- Please note the mixed use of knit and purl stitches in the cuff chart.
- Front and back of some fingers and thumbs have a different set of rounds repeating. Pay close attention to what round you are on.
- The Klivsi Glivs have also been made in an alternate colorway to match the Lund Socks. The charts are displayed in Colorway 1.

COLOR CHART

	Jamieson & Smith	Jamieson's of Shetland
Yarn A (MC)	Shade 9113 (Dark Red)	Shade 595 (Maroon)
Yarn B	Shade 5 (Dyed Shetland Black)	Shade 970 (Espresso)
Yarn C	Shade 4 (Moorit)	Shade 108 (Moorit)
Yarn D	Shade 28 (Mustard Yellow)	Shade 1160 (Scotch Broom)
Yarn E	Shade 66 (Medium Yellow)	Shade 182 (Buttercup)
Yarn F	Shade 53 (Peach)	Shade 440 (Peach)
Yarn G	Shade 1A (Natural White)	Shade 104 (Natural White)
Yarn H	Shade 142 (Dark Azure Blue)	Shade 750 (Petrol)

Cuff

Using A (MC), cast on 56 stitches, placing 28 sts on each of two needles to knit in the round, being careful not to twist your work. If using circular needles, pm to mark the beginning of the round.

Work Rounds 1–9 of Chart A using A (MC) and D, repeating the four-stitch repeat 14 times around. Repeat Rounds 6–9 three more times. Break off D.

Hand (Both Hands)

Round 1: Continuing with A (MC), knit to end of round.

Inc Round:

    Needle 1 (back of hand): K2, *KFB, K4; repeat from * to last st, K1.

    Needle 2 (palm of hand): K13, KFB, K14. *62 sts.*

Work Rounds 1–39 of the appropriate Hand Chart. See instructions below regarding thumb construction over Rounds 6–15 and decrease in Round 18.

Thumb Construction (Both Hands)

The thumb gusset starts with 5 sts, and this is gradually increased to 11 sts using M1R and M1L as indicated on chart. The green line on the charts indicates the 11 sts that will be picked up later to create the thumb. Work as per chart up to Round 15.

Round 16: When you get to the green line, knit the next 11 sts using a piece of waste yarn (it should be of contrasting color, so it stands out when you cut it). Move these 11 sts back onto the left-hand needle and work over them again in pattern as you continue to follow Round 16 of the Hand Chart. These 11 sts will be picked up later to create the thumb. After thumb increases you will have 68 sts.

Round 18: Work decrease (K2tog) in this round as marked. *67 sts.*

Hands Continued (Both Hands)

At the end of the hand chart, break off both colors.

Next Round: Rejoin A (MC) and knit to end of round.

Inc Round:

    Needle 1 (back of hand): K10, KFB, K10, KFB, K11.

    Needle 2 (palm of hand): K16, KFB, K17. *70 sts.*

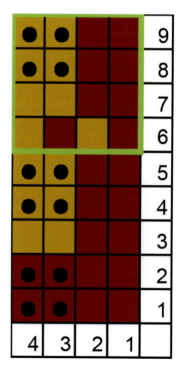

KEY:

• = *Purl*

/ = *M1R*

\ = *M1L*

X = *K2tog*

CHART A

RIGHT HAND CHART

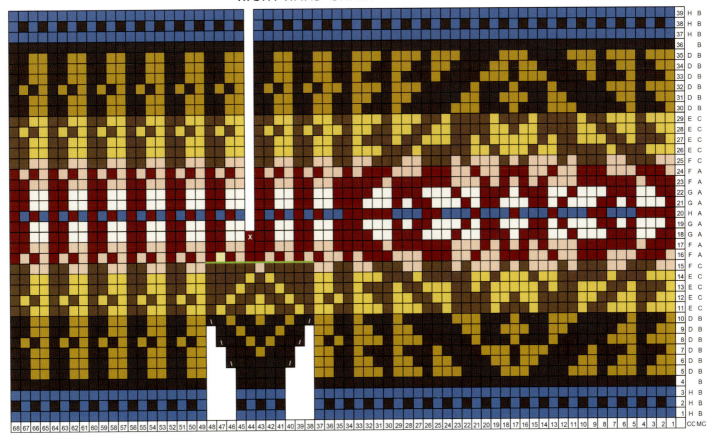

LEFT HAND CHART

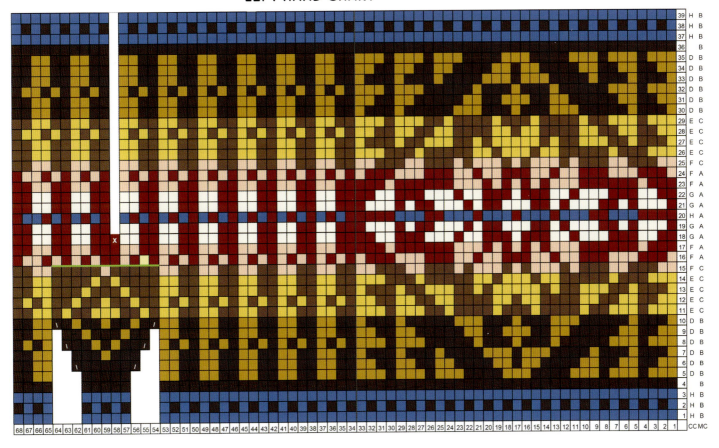

Fingers are worked in A and D.

Note: It is a good idea to leave a longish tail in A (MC) when starting to knit each finger, as this yarn can be used later to close any small gaps between fingers.

Little Finger (RH)

Setup: Without working any of the sts, slip the next 8 sts onto Needle 1, slip the next 54 sts onto stitch holders, and slip the last 8 sts onto Needle 2.

Round 1: With the back of the hand facing, work Round 1 of Chart B as follows: Pattern across sts 1–8, cast on 1 st with D, cast on 1 st with A, pattern across sts 11–18. *18 sts.*

Remaining Rounds: Repeat Rounds 1–4 [sts 1–8 (back of hand)] a total of four times (through Round 16), then work Rounds 17–21. Repeat Rounds 1–6 [sts 9–18 (palm of hand)] a total of three times (through Round 18), then work Rounds 19–21. Break both yarns and thread through the remaining 6 sts to close the fingertip. Tie securely on the inside and weave in the ends.

CHART B

KEY:
◊ = SKP

X = K2tog

⋀ = SK2P

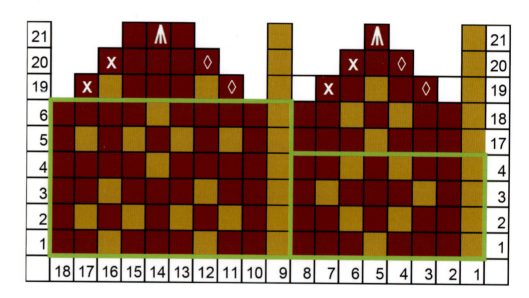

Ring Finger (RH)

Inc Round: Place remaining sts back onto the needles. Using A (MC) and with the back of the hand facing, M1L, K54, M1R. *56 sts.*

Setup: Without working any of the sts, slip the next 9 sts onto Needle 1, slip the next 38 sts onto stitch holders, slip the last 9 sts onto Needle 2.

Round 1: With the back of the hand facing, work Round 1 of Chart C as follows: Pick up and knit 1 st from the base of the last finger worked with D, pattern across sts 2–10, cast on 1 st with D, cast on 1 st with A, pattern across sts 13–21, pick up and knit 1 st from base of the last finger worked with A. *22 sts.*

Remaining Rounds: Repeat Rounds 1–6 a total of three times, then work Rounds 19–26. Break both yarns and thread through the remaining 6 sts to close the fingertip. Tie securely on the inside and weave in the ends.

CHART C

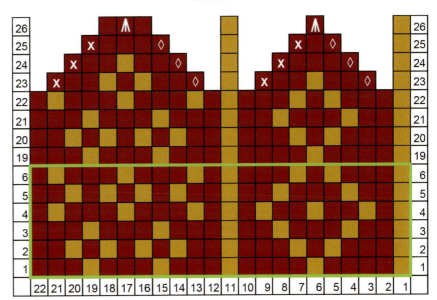

KEY:

◊ = *SKP*

X = *K2tog*

Λ = *SK2P*

Middle Finger (RH)

Setup: With the back of the hand facing and without working any of the sts, slip the next 9 sts onto Needle 1, slip the remaining 20 sts onto stitch holders, and slip the last 9 sts onto Needle 2.

Round 1: With the back of the hand facing, work Round 1 of Chart D as follows: Pick up and knit 1 st from the base of the last finger worked with D, pattern across sts 2–10, cast on 1 st with D, cast on 1 st with A, pattern across sts 13–21, pick up and knit 1 st from the base of the last finger worked with A. 22 *sts.*

Remaining Rounds: Repeat Rounds 1–6 a total of three times, then work Rounds 19–28. Break both yarns and thread through the remaining 6 sts to close the fingertip. Tie securely on the inside and weave in the ends.

CHART D

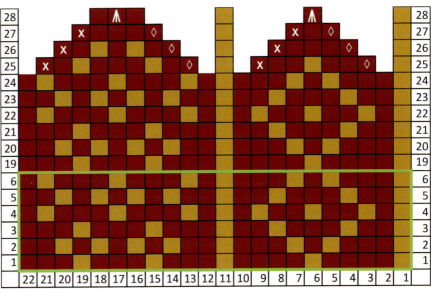

Index Finger (RH)

Place the remaining 20 sts onto your needles, with 10 sts on each needle.

Round 1: With the back of the hand facing, work Round 1 of Chart C as follows: Pick up and knit 1 st from the base of the last finger worked with D, pattern across sts 2–21, pick up and knit 1 st from the base of the last finger worked with A. 22 *sts.*

Remaining Rounds:

Follow the directions for Ring Finger (RH) for the remaining rounds.

Fingers: Left Hand

Break the yarn and turn your work so that the palm side is facing before proceeding to the fingers on the Left Hand.

Little Finger (LH)

Setup: Without working any of the stitches, slip 8 sts onto Needle 1, slip the next 54 sts onto stitch holders, and slip the last 8 sts onto Needle 2.

Round 1: With the palm of the hand facing, work Round 1 of Chart E as follows: pattern across sts 1–8, cast on 2 sts with A, pattern across sts 11 – 18. *18 sts.*

Remaining Rounds: Repeat Rounds 1–6 [sts 1–10 (palm of hand)] a total of three times (through Round 18), then work Rounds 19–21. Repeat Rounds 1–4 [sts 10–18 (back of hand)] a total of four times (through Round 16), then work Rounds 17–21. Break both yarns and thread through the remaining 6 sts to close the fingertip. Tie securely on the inside and weave in the ends.

CHART E

KEY:
◊ = SKP

X = K2tog

⋀ = SK2P

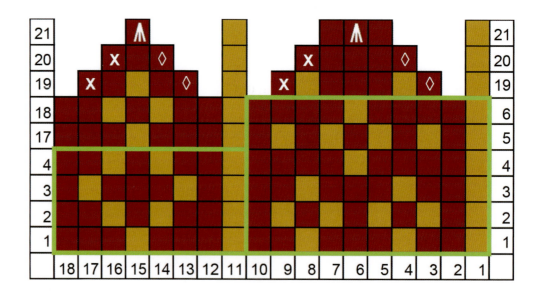

Ring Finger (LH)

Inc Round: Place the remaining sts back on to the needles. Using A and with the palm of the hand facing, M1L, K54, M1R. *56 sts.*

Setup: Without working any of the sts, slip the next 9 sts onto Needle 1, slip the next 38 sts onto stitch holders, slip the last 9 sts onto Needle 2.

Round 1: With the palm of the hand facing, work Round 1 of Chart F as follows: Pick up and knit 1 st from the base of the last finger worked with D, pattern across sts 2–10, cast on 2 sts with A, pattern across sts 13–21, pick up and knit 1 st from the base of the last finger worked with A. *22 sts.*

Remaining Rounds: Repeat Rounds 1–6 a total of three times, then work Rounds 19–26. Break both yarns and thread through the remaining 6 sts to close the fingertip. Tie securely on the inside and weave in the ends.

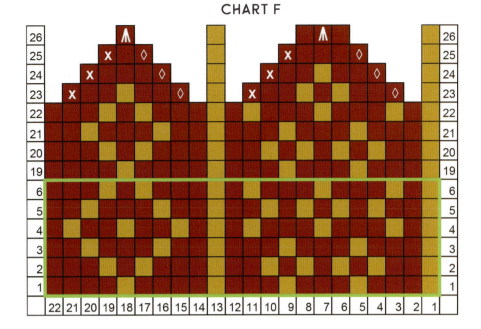

CHART F

KEY:

◊ = SKP

X = K2tog

Λ = SK2P

Middle Finger (LH)

Setup: With the palm of the hand facing and without working any of the sts, slip the next 9 sts onto Needle 1, slip the remaining 20 sts onto stitch holders, slip the last 9 sts onto Needle 2.

Round 1: With the palm of the hand facing, work Round 1 of Chart G as follows: Pick up and knit 1 st from the base of the last finger worked with D, pattern across sts 2–10, cast on 2 sts with A, pattern across sts 13–21, pick up and knit 1 st from the base of the next finger with A. *22 sts.*

Remaining Rounds: Repeat Rounds 1–6 a total of three times, then work Rounds 19–28. Break both yarns and thread through the remaining 6 sts to close the fingertip. Tie securely on the inside and weave in the ends.

KEY:
◊ = *SKP*

X = *K2tog*

⋀ = *SK2P*

Chart G (columns numbered bottom edge, left to right): 22 21 20 19 18 17 16 15 14 13 12 11 10 9 8 7 6 5 4 3 2 1

(rows numbered on left and right edges): 28, 27, 26, 25, 24, 23, 22, 21, 20, 19, 6, 5, 4, 3, 2, 1

Index Finger (LH)

Place the remaining 20 sts onto your needles, with 10 sts on each needle.

Round 1: With the palm of the hand facing, work Round 1 of Chart F as follows: Pick up and knit 1 st from the base of the last finger worked with D, pattern across sts 2–21, pick up and knit 1 st from the base of the next finger with A. *22 sts*.

Remaining Rounds: Follow the directions for Ring Finger (LH) for remaining rounds.

INSTRUCTIONS CONTINUED

Thumbs (Both Hands)

Setup: Without working sts, starting at the lower edge, pick up the right leg of the stitch just before the waste yarn, then pick up the 11 sts below the waste yarn, followed by one more after the waste yarn. Turn your work upside down so that the upper side of the thumb is showing. Pick up the right leg of the stitch just before the waste yarn, the 11 sts above the waste yarn, followed by one more after the waste yarn. *26 sts.* Arrange your stitches ready to work in the round. Using sharp scissors, carefully snip out the waste yarn.

Rounds 1–28: Repeat Rounds 1–8 [sts 1–12 (front of thumb)] twice (through Round 16), then work Rounds 17–28. Repeat Rounds 1–6 [sts 13–26 (back of thumb)] a total of three times (through Round 18), then work Rounds 19–28. Break both yarns and thread through the remaining 6 sts to close the tip of the thumb. Tie securely on the inside and weave in the ends.

Repeat for the other thumb.

KEY:

◊ = *SKP*

X = *K2tog*

⋀ = *SK2P*

CHART H

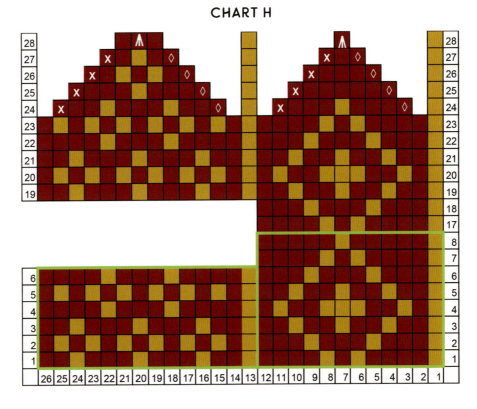

Finishing

Weave in ends. Close any small gaps that develop between the fingers or at the side of the thumb in the appropriate color.

Hand wash and rinse in warm water. Wrap in a towel to remove excess water or use a very light spin in a machine. Ideally, stretch on glove boards if you have them, or cover with damp towel and lightly steam press, pulling to shape.

VIRDIK VEST

Shetland has several high hills with variations of the name Virda or Virdik. These hills often have stacks of stones to mark the top. In the past, many of these have been burial sites or watch towers. It is said that fires could be lit on the top of the hill, acting as signals of warning. One high hill would always be in sight of another, allowing the alarm to spread very quickly around the isles in times of danger, especially war. One such hill is in Cunningsburgh, a place I still love to go, as I spent many happy days there as a child with my Nan.

YARN

- Jamieson & Smith 2ply Jumper Weight, 100% Shetland wool in 114 yards (105m)/25g balls.
- Yarns A and B: 4 (4, 5, 5, 6, 6) balls; Yarns C, D, E, and F: 2 (2, 3, 3, 3, 3) balls; Yarn G: 1 (1, 2, 2, 2, 2) ball(s), listed in the color chart.

NEEDLES

- US 2.5 (3mm) double-pointed needles (long) or preferred needles for working in the round. Adjust size if needed to obtain the correct tension.
- An extra needle will be needed for three-needle cast off if circular needles are used.

NOTIONS

- Stitch markers, stitch holders, tapestry needle.

TENSION

- 30 sts and 38 rounds to 4" x 4" (10 x 10cm), in stranded colorwork, after blocking. Please pay particular attention to the required tension and adjust needle size accordingly.

PATTERN NOTES

- The vest starts at the hem and is worked in the round to the armholes. Stitches are dropped at the armholes and steek sts are cast on to enable continuous working in the round. Stitches are dropped at the V-neck, and a steek is worked there also. The stitches are picked up at the armholes and are finished top-down with a section of corrugated ribbing.
- The design consists of horizontal Fair Isle motifs alternating between the peerie pattern (Chart B), and the two larger OXO patterns (Charts C and D). The size increments of the sweater are dictated by an additional horizontal repeat of the larger charts for each size. For example, Size 1 has eight Charts C in the round, Size 2 has nine, Size 3 has ten and so on.
- One of the important features of this vest is the centralization of the motifs so that they sit on top of each other and run up the middle in line with the V-neck. It is important, then, to locate the center stitch at the middle front and mark this with a stitch marker. As the front stitches are an even number, the center stitch will be the left one out of the two in the center. Stitch 7 of Chart B and stitch 19 of Charts C and D should always fall on this marked stitch. Because of this, the starting point for each size is different, so make sure you are careful to follow the instructions for your chosen size.
- Read all charts from right to left using the colors suggested or colors of your choosing.
- Steek stitches are not included in stitch counts.
- The charts are displayed in color with the addition of columns showing the pattern colors to the right of the chart. The background color is listed in the right column and the foreground color in the left column.

COLOR CHART

	Jamieson's of Shetland
Yarn A (MC)	Shade 82 (Dark Green)
Yarn B	Shade 32 (Bright Tan)
Yarn C	Shade FC45 (Tan)
Yarn D	Shade 28 (Mustard Yellow)
Yarn E	Shade 134 (Aubergine)
Yarn F	Shade 5 (Dyed Shetland Black)
Yarn G	Shade 91 (Egg Yolk Yellow)

FINISHED MEASUREMENTS

Sizes	1	2	3	4	5	6
Bust Circumference	38 ¾" (96cm)	43 ½" (108cm)	47" (119cm)	52" (132cm)	57" (145cm)	61 ½" (156cm)
Length (to underarm)	13" (33cm)	12 ½" (31.5cm)	11 ½" (29cm)	11" (28cm)	10 ½" (27cm)	10" (25.5cm)
Armhole Depth	7" (18cm)	7 ½" (19cm)	8 ½" (21.5cm)	9" (23cm)	9 ½" (24cm)	10" (25.5cm)
Cross Shoulder	16 ¼" (41cm)	16 ¾" (42.5cm)	17 ½" (44.5cm)	18" (46cm)	18 ½" (47cm)	19 ¼" (49cm)
V-Neck Depth	6 ½" (16.5cm)	6 ½" (16.5cm)	6 ½" (16.5cm)	6 ½" (16.5cm)	6 ½" (16.5cm)	6 ½" (16.5cm)
Back Neck Width	6 ½" (16.5cm)	7" (18cm)	7" (18cm)	7 ¼" (18.5cm)	7 ½" (19cm)	7 ½" (19cm)
Length	23 ½" (60cm)	23 ½" (60cm)	23 ½" (60cm)	23 ½" (60cm)	23 ½" (60cm)	23 ½" (60cm)

Using A (MC), cast on 252 (288, 320, 360, 384, 412) sts onto two needles and join to knit in the round, being careful not to twist the sts. Pm for the beginning of the round. The beginning of the round is located on the left side, so you will work across the front stitches first.

Corrugated Ribbing

Begin working from Round 1 of Chart A, working the four-stitch repeat 63 (72, 80, 90, 96, 103) times in total around. Continue working from Chart A as set, changing colors where indicated, until all 20 rounds are complete. Break off CC and continue in A (MC).
Round 21: Knit to end of round.

Sizes 1–5 Only:
   Inc Round: *K6 (7, 7, 9, 7), KFB; repeat from * to end of round. 288 (324, 360, 396, 432) sts.

Size 6 Only:
   Inc Round: K10, *K6, KFB; repeat from * to last 10 sts, K10. 468 sts.

All Sizes:
   Round 23: Knit to end of round.

Body

Arrange your stitches so that half are on the front and half are on the back. Place a marker between the front and back, on the right-hand side. Once the pattern is established, pm on the center front stitch (on stitch number 73 [82, 91, 100, 109, 118]). The starting point for each size is different, so make sure you are careful to follow the instructions for your chosen size.
Chart Sequence: Chart B, Chart C, Chart B, Chart D, repeated throughout the vest.

CHART A

4	3	2	1		CC	MC
•	•			20	B	A
•	•			19	B	A
•	•			18	B	A
•	•			17	B	A
•	•			16	C	A
•	•			15	C	A
•	•			14	C	A
•	•			13	C	A
•	•			12	D	A
•	•			11	D	A
•	•			10	D	A
•	•			9	D	A
•	•			8	C	A
•	•			7	C	A
•	•			6	C	A
•	•			5	C	A
•	•			4	B	A
•	•			3	B	A
•	•			2	B	A
•	•			1	B	A

KEY:
• = *Purl*

Peerie Band (Chart B)

Begin working from Round 1 of Chart B, beginning with stitch number 1 (10, 7, 4, 1, 10) of Chart B, working the 12-stitch repeat 24 (27, 30, 33, 36, 39) times in total around. Continue working from Chart B as set, changing colors where indicated, until all 13 rounds are complete.

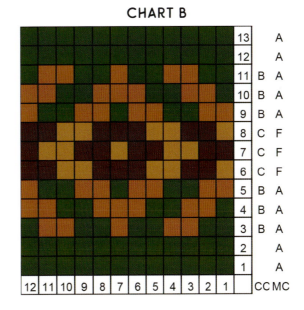

CHART B

Begin working from Round 1 of Chart C, beginning with stitch number 1 (10, 7, 4, 1, 10) of Chart C, working the 36-stitch repeat 8 (9, 10, 11, 12, 13) times in total around. Continue working from Chart C as set, changing colors where indicated, until all 19 rounds are complete.

Repeat the Peerie Band section once more.

Begin working from Round 1 of Chart D, beginning with stitch number 1 (10, 7, 4, 1, 10) of Chart D, working the 36-stitch repeat 8 (9, 10, 11, 12, 13) times in total around. Continue working from Chart D as set, changing colors where indicated, until all 19 rounds are complete.

Repeat Chart B, Chart C, then Rounds 1–13 (13, 13, 13, 13, 11) of Chart B.

Size 1 Only: Work Rounds 1–19 of Chart D, then Rounds 1–5 of Chart B.

Size 2 Only: Work Rounds 1–19 of Chart D, then Round 1 of Chart B.

Sizes 3–5 Only: Work Rounds 1–12 (8, 2) of Chart D. (Note: Be sure to work Chart B once, completing Chart D during the underarm shaping section.)

Size 6 Only: Proceed to Drop Underarms. (Note: Be sure to work Chart D once, completing Chart B during the underarm shaping section.)

CHART C

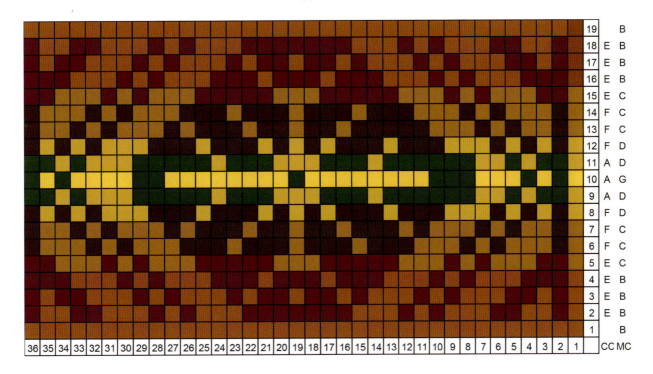

Drop Underarms

Note: The chart sequence for the armholes and neck:
- Sizes 1–2: Charts B/C/B/D/B
- Sizes 3–5: Charts D/B/C/B/D/B
- Size 6: Charts B/D/B/C/B/D/B

All sizes finish at the end of Chart B for the shoulder join. All sizes will begin the neck on a Round 13 of Chart B. Maintain the pattern as established, ensuring that all charts sit directly in line and on top of the previous charts. You will need to work out the starting stitch at the beginning of each round from the previous chart, as the armhole decreases change the starting point.

Next Round: Working in pattern, work 6 (10, 13, 16, 18, 22) sts and place them on a stitch holder, work across front to right-side marker, rm, then work the next 6 (10, 13, 16, 18, 22) sts, and place the 12 (20, 26, 32, 36, 44) sts just worked on a stitch holder, then work to end, and place the 6 (10, 13, 16, 18, 22) sts just worked on hold as well. *132 (142, 154, 166, 180, 190) front/back sts.*

Steek Setup Round: Work in pattern to side, pm, cast on 8 steek sts as: [K1 MC, K1 CC] twice, [K1 CC, K1 MC] twice, pm, work in pattern to end, and cast on another 8 steek sts as above, placing a marker before and after the steek sts. The beginning of the round is now between the steek sts and the front sts (at the left underarm), but change any colors in the middle of the steek, between sts 4 and 5 of the left underarm steek. If using DPNs, the 8 steek sts can be divided to put four on each needle once they have been knitted over. *132 (142, 154, 166, 180, 190) front/back sts.*

Note: Steek stitches are not included in any of the remaining stitch counts.

Dec Round: [K1, SKP, work to marker, sm, work steek, sm] twice. *131 (141, 153, 165, 179, 189) front/back sts.* This decrease round ensures that edge sts are symmetrical on both sides of the armholes.

CHART D

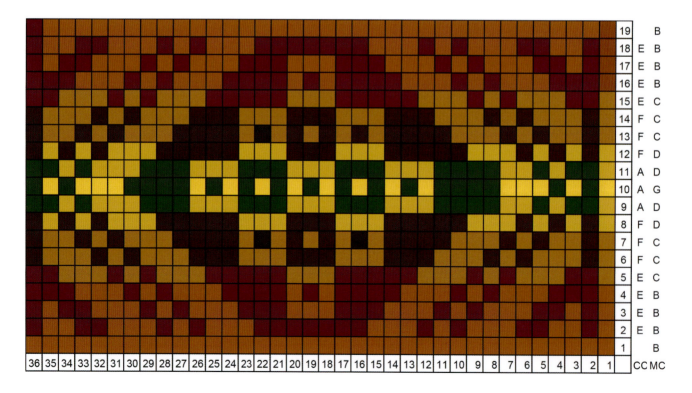

Armhole Shaping

Armhole Dec Round: [K1, SKP, work to 3 sts before marker, K2tog, K1, sm, work steek] twice. *4 sts dec.* Work the Armhole Dec Round every other round 1 (3, 4, 6, 9, 11) more times, ending with a plain (no decreases) round. *127 (133, 143, 151, 159, 165) front/back sts.*

Sizes 1 and 2 Only:
   Neck Separation Round: On Round 13 of Chart B, work to marked center st, then take this stitch off your needles and place it on a stitch holder. Pm and cast on 8 steek sts as: [K1 MC, K1 CC] twice, [K1 CC, K1 MC] twice, pm, then continue in pattern to end. *63 (65) sts on each front.*
   Then work Round 1 of Chart C. Proceed to Armhole and V-Neck Shaping.

Sizes 3–6 Only:
   Work the Armhole Dec Round every 4th round once. Work three rounds in pattern with no decreases, then work the following round on Round 13 of Chart B:
   Neck Separation and Armhole Dec Round: K1, SKP, work to marked center st, then take this stitch off your needles and place it on a stitch holder. Pm and cast on 8 steek sts as: [K1 MC, K1 CC] twice, [K1 CC, K1 MC] twice, pm, work to 3 sts before side, K2tog, K1, sm, work steek, sm, K1, SKP, work to 3 sts before side, K2tog, K1, sm, work steek. *139 (147, 155, 161) back sts, 69 (73, 77, 80) sts on each front.*
   Then work Round 1 of Chart C. Proceed to Armhole and V-Neck Shaping.

Armhole and V-Neck Shaping

Sizes 1 and 2 Only:
   Work an Armhole and V-Neck Dec Round (page 138) on next round, then work one round in pattern with no decreases. Work a V-Neck Dec Round (page 138), then work one round in pattern with no decreases.
   Repeat the last four rounds 1 (2) more times. *123 (127) back sts, 57 (57) sts on each front.*
   Then work a V-Neck Dec Round every other round 20 (19) more times, or until 37 (38) sts remain on the front shoulders. Proceed to Join Shoulders.

Sizes 3–6 Only:
   Work a V-Neck Dec Round (page 138) on the next round, then work one round in pattern with no decreases. Work an Armhole and V-Neck Dec Round (page 138), then work one round in pattern with no decreases.
   Repeat the last four rounds 2 (4, 6, 6) more times. *133 (137, 141, 147) back sts, 60 (58, 56, 59) sts on each front.*
   Then work a V-Neck Dec Round every other round 20 (17, 14, 14) more times, or until 40 (41, 42, 45) sts remain on the front shoulders. Proceed to Join Shoulders.

Armhole and V-Neck Dec Round: K1, SKP, work in pattern to 3 sts before V-neck steek, K2tog, K1, sm, work steek, sm, *K1, SKP, work in pattern to last 3 sts before armhole steek, K2tog, K1, sm, work steek, sm; repeat from * once more. *6 sts dec.*

V-Neck Dec Round: Work in pattern to 3 sts before V-neck steek, K2tog, K1, sm, work steek, sm, K1, SKP, work in pattern to end. *2 sts dec.*

Join Shoulders

Continue without shaping until Round 9 of Chart B is complete (about 12 [10, 8, 6, 4, 4] more rounds). Do not break the yarn.

Round 10 (of Chart B): Cast off 4 steek sts at the beginning of the round. Knit 37 (38, 40, 41, 42, 45) sts of left front shoulder, maintaining Chart B pattern, cast off 8 steek sts at V-neck, knit 37 (38, 40, 41, 42, 45) sts of right front shoulder, maintaining Chart B pattern, cast off 8 steek sts at the right sleeve, knit 37 (38, 40, 41, 42, 45) sts across right back shoulder, place the next 49 (51, 53, 55, 57, 57) sts onto a stitch holder for the back neck, knit the last 37 (38, 40, 41, 42, 45) across left back shoulder, and cast off remaining 4 steek sts.

From here on, work each of the four shoulders separately. You can either break and rejoin the yarns to continue working from the right side (known as brak and eke), or you can keep the yarns intact and purl the even-numbered rows.

All Shoulders: Knit Rows 11 and 12. Store sts on stitch holder.

Turn your work inside out and, using A (MC), join the front and back shoulder sections using the three-needle cast-off method .

Cut the V-neck and armhole steek sts down the middle. Curl the edges under and, taking a length of MC yarn, stitch the edges in place. Follow the line of the outermost steek stitch (which should always be in MC), making sure that each knitted stitch is held securely with a sewn stitch.

Neck Ribbing

With RS facing, using A (MC), and beginning at left shoulder seam, pick up and knit 56 (57, 56, 57, 58, 58) sts down left front neck to held stitch, knit center stitch (pm here or loop some yarn around the stitch before knitting it to mark it), pick up and knit 56 (57, 56, 57, 58, 58) sts up right front neck, pick up and knit 3 sts from right back, knit across 49 (51, 53, 55, 57, 57) sts from back neck on holder, pick up and knit 3 sts from left back. *167 (171, 171, 175, 179, 179) sts.*

Round 1: Work two-colored corrugated ribbing setup as follows: [K2 A, K2 B], but stop 5 sts before center st at V-neck, K2 A, K1 B, SKP B, K center st with A, K2tog B, K1 B, K2 A, then continue (reversing patterning before center st) in [K2 B, K2 A] to end of round. *165 (169, 169, 173, 177, 177) sts.*

Rounds 2 and 3: Continue working established ribbing as follows: [K2 A, P2 B], but continue to decrease by P2tog on either side of center neck stitch on Round 3 using the appropriate color for the two-colored rib. The center st should be knitted in A on every round. *163 (167, 167, 171, 175, 175) sts.*

Rounds 4–6: Continue working established ribbing as follows: [K2 A, P2 C], but continue to decrease by P2tog on either side of center neck stitch on Round 5 using the appropriate color for the two-colored rib. The center st should be knitted in A on every round. *161 (165, 165, 169, 173, 173) sts.*

Rounds 7–9: Continue working established ribbing as follows: [K2 A, P2 B], but continue to decrease by P2tog on either side of center neck stitch on Rounds 7, 8, and 9 using the appropriate color for the two-colored rib. The center st should be knitted in A on every round. *155 (159, 159, 163, 167, 167) sts.*

Using A (MC), cast off neatly in ribbing.

Arm Ribbing

Work the arm ribbing beginning from the center of the underarm.

With RS of work facing and using A (MC), knit across 6 (10, 13, 16, 18, 22) sts from needle holder, pick up and knit 56 (60, 69, 72, 78, 82) sts from back armhole up to shoulder seam, pick up and knit 56 (60, 69, 72, 78, 82) down front armhole, then knit across remaining 6 (10, 13, 16, 18, 22) underarm sts on needle holder. *124 (140, 164, 176, 192, 208) sts.*

Place marker and begin working in the round.

Round 1: Work two-color corrugated ribbing as follows: [K2 A, K2 B] to end of round.

Rounds 2–4: Continue working corrugated ribbing as follows: [K2 A, P2 B] to end of round.

Rounds 5–7: Continue working corrugated ribbing as follows: [K2 A, P2 C] to end of round.

Rounds 8–10: Continue working corrugated ribbing as follows: [K2 A, P2 B] to end of round.

Using A (MC), cast off neatly in ribbing.

Repeat for second armhole.

Finishing

Weave in all the ends. Using warm water and a small amount of wool wash, submerge the garment, leaving until the water is absorbed and squeeze gently (do not wring). Using fresh water, rinse twice before rolling in a towel to remove excess water (or use a very light spin in a washing machine). Stretch the vest on a jumper board if you have one and leave to dry. Otherwise, dry flat on a blocking mat or clean, dry towels. Pull to shape. If ribbing becomes too stretched, this can be pulled in again by using steam, if necessary.

UMSKET GANSEY

Umsket Gansey is a traditional Fair Isle gansey with horizontal bands of alternating large and peerie patterns. A common feature in Fair Isle knitting is to use diamond shading as an effective and gentle way to change the background color from dark to light. This technique has been around since around the 1920s but was a regular feature in the ganseys we all wore to school in the 1970s.

I like to use such traditional techniques in my designs, as I have a fondness for vintage designs, but also to honor and acknowledge the expert knitters of that time who created and developed Fair Isle knitting into what it is today. In this design, I use natural shades with some dyed dusky pinks and reds to add color and interest. *Umsket* is an adjective Shetlanders would use to describe something dusky in color.

YARN

- Jamieson & Smith Supreme Jumper Weight, 100% Shetland wool in 199 yards (182m)/50g balls.
- Yarn A: 4 (4, 5, 6) balls; Yarn B: 2 (2, 3, 3) balls; Yarn D: 3 (3, 4, 4) balls, listed in the color chart.
- Jamieson & Smith 2ply Jumper Weight, 100% Shetland wool in 114 yards (105m)/25g balls.
- Yarn C: 3 (3, 4, 4) balls; Yarn E: 2 (2, 3, 3) balls; Yarns F and G: 1 (1, 2, 2) ball(s) of each, listed in the color chart.

NEEDLES

- US 2.5 (3mm) double-pointed needles (long) or preferred needles for working in the round. Adjust size if needed to obtain the correct tension.
- An extra needle will be needed for three-needle cast off if circular needles are used.

NOTIONS

- Stitch markers, stitch holders, tapestry needle.

TENSION

- 32 sts and 40 rounds to 4" x 4" (10 x 10cm), in stranded colorwork, after blocking. Please pay particular attention to the required tension and adjust needle size accordingly.

PATTERN NOTES

- The gansey starts at the hem and is worked in the round to the armholes. Stitches are dropped at the armholes and steek stitches are cast on to enable continuous working in the round. Stitches are dropped at the neck and a steek is worked there also. The sleeves are then picked up and worked top-down, finishing with corrugated ribbing at the cuffs. The crew neck features corrugated ribbing.
- Steek stitches are not included in stitch counts.
- Work all charts from right to left using the colors suggested or colors of your choosing.

COLOR CHART

	Jamieson & Smith
Yarn A (MC)	Shade 2005 (Shetland Black)
Yarn B	Shade 2004 (Moorit)
Yarn C	Shade 78 (Dark Fawn)
Yarn D	Shade 2006 (Gaulmogit)
Yarn E	Shade 9113 (Dark Red)
Yarn F	Shade 72 (Mid Salmon Pink)
Yarn G	Shade 66 (Medium Yellow)

FINISHED MEASUREMENTS

Sizes	1	2	3	4
Bust Circumference	35 ½" (90cm)	41 ½" (105cm)	47" (119cm)	53" (135cm)
Length (to underarm)	14 ½" (37cm)	14 ½" (37cm)	13 ½" (34cm)	12 ½" (32cm)
Armhole Depth	8" (20.5cm)	8" (20.5cm)	9 ½" (24cm)	10" (25.5cm)
Cross Shoulder	14 ½" (37cm)	15 ½" (39cm)	18" (46cm)	19" (48cm)
Upperarm Circumference	17" (43cm)	17 ½" (44.5cm)	21" (53cm)	23 ½" (60cm)
Cuff Circumference	8 ½" (21.5cm)	8 ½" (21.5cm)	9" (23cm)	9" (23cm)
Sleeve Length	20" (51cm)	20" (51cm)	20" (51cm)	20" (51cm)
Back Neck Width	5 ½" (14cm)	5 ½" (14cm)	6 ¼" (16cm)	6 ¾" (17cm)
Neck Circumference	15 ¾" (40cm)	15 ¾" (40cm)	17 ½" (44.5cm)	18 ½" (47cm)
Length	23" (58cm)	23" (58cm)	23" (58cm)	23" (58cm)

Using A (MC), cast on 240 (280, 320, 360) sts and join to knit in the round, being careful not to twist the sts. The beginning of the round is located on the left side, so you will work across the front stitches first. Pm after stitch number 120 (140, 160, 180), between the front and back, on the right side.

Corrugated Ribbing

Round 1: *K2A, K2E; repeat from * to end of round.
Rounds 2–5: *K2A, P2E; repeat from * to end of round.
Rounds 6–8: *K2A, P2F; repeat from * to end of round.
Rounds 9–15: Work Rounds 9–15 in pattern as shown on Chart A.
Rounds 16–18: *K2A, P2F; repeat from * to end of round.
Rounds 19–23: *K2A, P2E; repeat from * to end of round.
Break off CC and continue with A (MC).
Round 24: Knit to end of round.
Inc Round: *K4, KFB; repeat from * to end of round. *48 (56, 64, 72) sts increased, 288 (336, 384, 432) sts.*
Rounds 26–28: Knit to end of round.

Body

Note: Only sizes 1 and 3 will begin working Charts B and C from stitch number 13, in order to center the motif in the center front and back. Sizes 2 and 4 will begin with stitch number 1.

All Sizes: Work Rounds 1–60 of Chart B once.
Sizes 1 and 2 Only: Work Rounds 1–60 of Chart C once.
Size 3 Only: Work Rounds 1–46 of Chart C.
Size 4 Only: Work Rounds 1–38 of Chart C.

CHART A

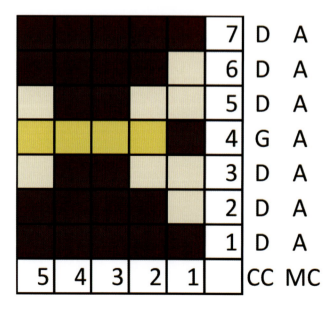

CHART B

Drop Underarms

Begin working from Chart B (B, C, C) with Round 1 (1, 47, 39).

Next Round: K10 (13, 18, 23) sts and place on needle holder, work in pattern across front to marker, remove marker, then work the next 10 (13, 18, 23) sts in pattern, and place the 20 (26, 36, 46) sts just worked on needle holder, then work in pattern to end, and place the last 10 (13, 18, 23) sts just worked on hold as well. Break and secure both yarns. *124 (142, 156, 170) front/back sts.*

Note: Steek stitches are not included in any of the remaining stitch counts.

Next Round: Rejoin yarns and work in pattern across front sts, maintaining the pattern as established, pm. Cast on 8 steek sts at right underarm as: [K1 MC, K1 CC] twice, [K1 CC, K1 MC] twice, pm, then work across back sts and at the end of the round cast on another 8 steek sts as above, pm before and after the steek sts. Beginning of round is now between the steek sts and the front sts but change any colors in the middle of the steek, between sts 4 and 5 of the left armhole steek.

Continue working in pattern, and begin armhole edge shaping:

If using DPNs, the 8 steek sts can be divided to put 4 on each needle once they have been knitted over.

Next Round (Dec): *K1, K2tog, work in pattern to end of front sts, sm, work steek, sm; repeat from * once more across back. *2 sts dec, 123 (141, 155, 169) front/back sts.*

This decrease round ensures that edge sts are symmetrical on both sides of the armholes.

Armhole Decreases

You will now begin decreases at the armholes.

Work 2 rounds in pattern.

Dec Round: *K1, SKP, knit to 3 sts before armhole steek, K2tog, K1, sm, work steek, sm; repeat from * once more across back. *4 sts dec.*

Work Dec Round every 3rd round 2 (7, 4, 7) more times—switching to working Chart B for Sizes 3 and 4 when finishing Chart C. *117 (125, 145, 153) front/back sts.*

Work in pattern through Round 59 of Chart B.

Neck

Next Round: Work 40 (44, 51, 53) sts across front of Chart B. Place the next 37 (37, 43, 47) sts on a stitch holder. Pm and cast on 8 steek sts as: [K1 MC, K1 CC] twice, [K1 CC, K1 MC] twice, pm, then work in pattern to end of round. *40 (44, 51, 53) sts on either side of neck.*

Next Round: Start working again from Round 1 of Chart C, working pattern as set to end.

Next Round: Work in pattern to 3 sts from first marker, K2tog, K1, sm, work steek, sm, K1, SKP, work in pattern to end. *2 sts dec.*

Next Round: Work in pattern to end.

Repeat last two rounds three more times, until 36 (40, 47, 49) sts remain on each front shoulder.

Continue without shaping until Round 18 of Chart C is complete. Do not break yarn.

CHART C

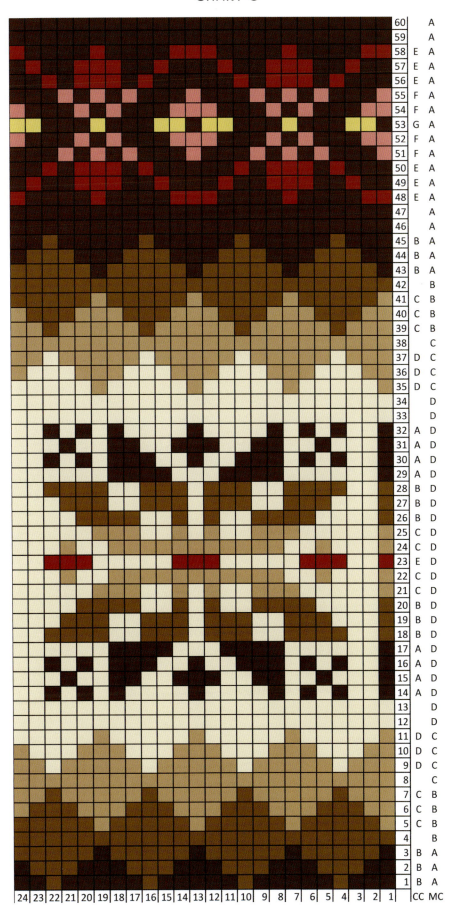

Join Shoulders

Next Round: Removing markers as you come to them, cast off 4 steek sts at the beginning of the round. Work 36 (40, 47, 49) sts of Left Front shoulder, maintaining Chart C pattern, cast off 8 steek sts at neck, work 36 (40, 47, 49) sts of Right Front shoulder, maintaining Chart C pattern, cast off 8 steek sts at the Right Sleeve, work 36 (40, 47, 49) sts across Right Back shoulder, place the next 45 (45, 51, 55) sts onto a needle holder for the back neck, work the last 36 (40, 47, 49) across Left Back shoulder, and cast off remaining 4 steek sts. From here on, work each of the four shoulders separately. You can either break and rejoin the yarns to continue working from the right side (known as brak and eke), or you can keep the yarns intact and purl the even-numbered rows.

Left and Right Front: Work Rows 20–22. Store sts on needle holder.

Right and Left Back: Work Rows 20–23. Store sts on needle holder.

Turn your work inside out and, using A (MC), join the front and back shoulder sections using the three-needle cast-off method (making sure that the two halves of the pattern on each side meet).

Cut the neck and armhole steek sts down the middle. Curl the edges under and, taking a length of MC yarn, stitch the edges in place. Follow the line of the outermost steek stitch (which should always be in MC), making sure that each knitted stitch is held securely with a sewn stitch.

Sleeves

Work the sleeves beginning from the center of the underarm.

Right {Left} Sleeve

With RS of work facing and using A (MC), knit across 10 (13, 18, 23) sts from needle holder, pick up and knit 59 (59, 67, 73) sts from back {front} armhole up to shoulder seam, pick up and knit 58 (58, 66, 72) down front {back} armhole, then knit across remaining 10 (13, 18, 23) underarm sts on needle holder. *137 (143, 169, 191) sts.*

Chart Order

Chart C, Chart B, followed by Chart C again (all knitted in reverse round order, starting at Round 60 and working down to Round 1).

Begin working Chart C with stitch number 17 (14, 25, 14) in order to center the design on the sleeve.

Pm and begin working in the round. Begin at Round 60 of Chart C, working the charts in the reverse order (starting at Round 60 and working down the sleeve to Round 1). Work Rounds 60–51 of Chart C without decreases. Decreases start on Round 50 of Chart C as follows:

Decreases

Dec Round 1: K2tog, work in pattern to last 3 sts, SKP, K1. *2 sts dec.*
Work Dec Round 1 every 6th (6th, 4th, 4th) round 21 (6, 35, 2) more times, then every 5th (5th, 3rd, 3rd) round 7 (25, 7, 51) times. *79 (79, 83, 83) sts.*
Work in pattern (about 8 more rounds) until Round 1 of Chart C has been completed.
Next Round: Using A (MC), knit 1 round.
Dec Round 2: K6 (6, 10, 10), K2tog, *K5, K2tog; repeat from * to last st, K1. *68 (68, 72, 72) sts.*

Cuff

Knit 18 rounds of 2x2 Corrugated Ribbing as follows. The cuff is also shown in Chart D.
Round 1: *K2A, K2E; repeat from * to end of round.
Rounds 2–7: *K2A, P2E; repeat from * to end of round.
Rounds 8–12: *K2A, P2F; repeat from * to end of round.
Rounds 13–18: *K2A, P2E; repeat from * to end of round.
Using A (MC), cast off in ribbing.
Complete Left Sleeve as for Right Sleeve.

Neck Ribbing

With RS facing, using A (MC) and beginning at left shoulder seam, pick up and knit 21 sts down left front neck, knit 37 (37, 43, 47) sts from front neck on holder, pick up and knit 21 sts up right front neck, pick up and knit 2 sts from right back, knit across 45 (45, 51, 55) sts from back neck on holder, 2 sts from left back. *128 (128, 140, 148) sts.*
Work Corrugated Ribbing for a total of 8 rounds as follows:
Round 1: *K2A, K2E; repeat from * to end of round.
Rounds 2 and 3: *K2A, P2E; repeat from * to end of round.
Rounds 4 and 5: *K2A, P2F; repeat from * to end of round.
Rounds 6–8: *K2A, P2E; repeat from * to end of round. Using A (MC), cast off in ribbing, being careful to not cast off too tightly.

Finishing

Weave in all the ends. Using warm water and a small amount of wool wash, submerge the garment, leaving until the water is absorbed and squeeze gently (do not wring). Using fresh water, rinse twice before rolling in a towel to remove excess water (or use a very light spin in a washing machine). Stretch gansey on a jumper board if you have one and leave to dry. Otherwise, dry flat on a blocking mat or clean, dry towels. Pull to shape. If ribbing becomes too stretched, this can be pulled in again using steam, if necessary.

KEY:
• = *Purl*

CHART D

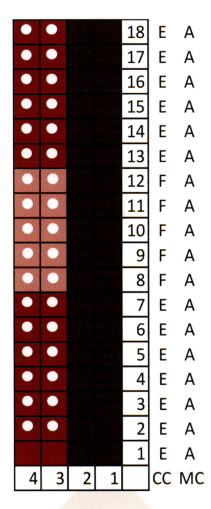

4	3	2	1		CC	MC

(Rows, top to bottom: 18 E A, 17 E A, 16 E A, 15 E A, 14 E A, 13 E A, 12 F A, 11 F A, 10 F A, 9 F A, 8 F A, 7 E A, 6 E A, 5 E A, 4 E A, 3 E A, 2 E A, 1 E A)

ABBREVIATIONS

*   repeat directions listed after asterisks the indicated number of times

[ ]   repeat directions listed between brackets the indicated number of times

CC   contrast color

CDD   center double decrease; slip 2 stitches knitwise, K1, pass the slipped stitches over the knitted stitch (*2 sts dec*)

dec   decrease(d)

DPN(s) double pointed needle(s)

inc   increase(d)

K   knit

K2tog knit 2 sts together as if they were 1 stitch (*1 st dec*)

K3tog knit 3 sts together as if they were 1 stitch (*2 sts dec*)

KFB   knit into the front and then into the back of a stitch (*1 st inc*)

LH   left hand

LS   left side

M1L   make one left; lift the bar between sts from front to back and knit through the back of this loop (*1 left-leaning st inc*)

M1R   make one right; lift the bar between sts from back to front and knit through the front of this loop (*1 right-leaning st inc*)

MC   main color

P   purl

P2tog purl 2 together (*1 st dec*)

pm   place marker

RH   right hand

rm   remove marker

RS   right side

SKP   slip, knit, pass over; slip the next stitch, knit 1 stitch, pass the slipped st over the knitted st (*1 st dec*)

SK2P slip, knit 2, pass over; slip the next stitch, knit next 2 stitches together, pass the slipped st over the knitted together sts (*2 sts dec*)

sl   slip as if to purl

sm   slip marker

st(s) stitch(es)

tbl   through back of loop

WS   wrong side

wyib with yarn in back

wyif with yarn in front

yo   yarnover

KEY:

B = *Work stitch in both colors*

X = *K2tog*

\ = *M1L*

/ = *M1R*

• = *Purl*

Δ = *CDD*

+ = *Slip purlwise with yarn at back*

± = *Slip purlwise with yarn at front*

◊ = *SKP*

Λ = *SK2P*

BIBLIOGRAPHY

Abrams, Lyann, Roslyn Chapman, Carol Christiansen, Martin Ciszuk, Sarah Dearlove, Lena Hammarlund, Elizabeth Johnston, Sarah Laurenson, and Brian Smith. *Shetland Textiles 800 BC to the Present*. Lerwick, UK: Shetland Amenity Trust, 2013.

Angus, James Stout. *A Glossary of the Shetland Dialect*. Los Angeles: Hardpress Publishing, 1914. https://archive.org/details/cu31924026538979.

Fryer, Linda G. *Knitting by The Fireside and on the Hillside: A History of the Shetland Hand Knitting Industry c. 1600–1950*. Lerwick, UK: Shetland Times Ltd, 1995.

Jakobsen, Jakob. *The Dialect and Place Names of Shetland: Two Popular Lectures*. London: Forgotten Books, 2018. First published 1897 by T. & J. Manson (Lerwick, UK).

Jamieson's of Shetland. "About Us." https://www.jamiesonsofshetland.co.uk/about-us-1-w.asp.

Jamieson & Smith. "About Us." https://www.shetlandwoolbrokers.co.uk/about-us.

Livingstone, W. P. *Shetland and the Shetlanders*. Edinburgh: Thomas Nelson & Sons, 1947.

McGregor, Sheila. *The Complete Book of Traditional Fair Isle Knitting*. London: B. T. Batsford Ltd, 1981.

Saxby, Jessie M. E. *Shetland Traditional Lore*. Edinburgh: Grant & Murray, 1932.

Shetland ForWirds. https://www.shetlanddialect.org.uk.

Shetland Sheep Society. https://www.shetland-sheep.org.uk.

Uradale Yarns. "About Our Yarn." https://www.uradale.com/pages/about-our-yarn.

INDEX

Note: Page numbers in *italics* indicate projects.

ABOUT THE AUTHOR

A Shetlander born and bred, **Alison Rendall** is a designer of hand-knitting patterns who cherishes traditional techniques. She grew up in the early 1970s surrounded by knitters in Shetland, and learned to knit when she was very young, being taught in school at eight or nine.

She is a proud supporter of Shetland's heritage and very involved in Shetland Wool Week, not only creating online content for that event, but also having been named the 2023 patron. Wool Week is a world-renowned celebration of Britain's most northerly native sheep, the Shetland textile industry, and the rural crafting community on these small islands. Alison's work is stunningly authentic, and through social media and Ravelry, she is growing a significant fanbase in the knitting community. Her pattern line includes pullover knits, slippers, ankle socks, gloves, beanies, scarves, and hats. She is also a trained nurse. *Fair Isle Knitting Tradition* is her first book.

ACKNOWLEDGMENTS

Thanks to all my family and friends who have supported me in writing this book. I'd like to thank my husband for his patience, advice, and photography. Thanks to my mother for her help with proofreading and factchecking. Thanks also to my models, four of whom are my grownup children, and to the two "peerie lasses" for modelling the children's hats. Finally, thanks to the Shetland knitting community that I am proud to be part of.

Kevin Theakston: photography
Isobel Rendall: proofreading
Katya Moncrieff: model
Lyla Moncrieff: model
Alec Moncrieff: model
Nina Moncrieff: model
Penny Williamson: model
Lyndi Robertson: model